Quick

Italian

Diethard Lübke

TEACH YOURSELF BOOKS
Hodder and Stoughton

Contents

Introduction

How to Speak Italian

Introduction to Italian Grammar

Contents

Introduction

This course of self study aims to help you understand and speak simple Italian, the sort of Italian you will need on a visit to Italy. It cannot promise that at the end you will be speaking perfectly, but by enabling you to learn the most important words and expressions a visitor needs, it will undoubtedly help to improve your experience of Italy and get more out of your time abroad.

The course does not require a great deal of study or concentration, but it does offer more than a phrase-book and you will find that if you are prepared to spend a certain amount of time, even at odd hours of the day, in going through each unit in turn and testing your knowledge carefully, you will begin to acquire a basic knowledge of the language. Then take the book with you on your trip abroad, so that you can practise the words and phrases you have learnt. Don't be afraid to use them – you are bound to make mistakes, but the most important thing is that you will have made yourself understood.

The course consists of 20 units, each dealing with a particular aspect of a visit to Italy. Within each unit are groups of words and phrases with English translations. Look at them carefully and read them aloud, referring where necessary to the Pronunciation section. The exercises which follow are of two types: those which require a test of memory, to see if you have remembered how to ask a question or say a phrase which has occurred on the previous page, and those which ask you to adapt a given phrase or sentence to suit your *own* purposes. For example, in Unit 9, on the subject of shopping, you will find the expression **Mi piace questa camicia** (*I like this shirt*). Turn the page and you will find you are asked to state that you like a particular handbag, and in Unit 13 you are asked to state that you like certain foods. If you can do this, you have passed the 'acid test' of learning a language, which is being able to adapt given language patterns to any situation you choose.

At the end of each unit is a short information section in English which you will find useful on your visit.

The course expects very little knowledge of grammar, but readers who are interested in learning *how* the language works will find the introduction to Italian grammar useful. This contains brief description of some of the basic elements of grammar, mainly those which are illustrated in the course. A careful study of the Pronunciation section is essential, because, although there can be no substitute for listening to Italians talk their own language, it is possible to give a fairly good approximation of individual sounds. It is a good idea to read both these sections before starting the course, and then to refer back to them frequently.

How to Speak Italian

The following guidelines may be useful:

1 In Italian one syllable of each word is always stressed more than the others. Most words have their stress on the syllable *before* the last: banca, signore. There are, however, some words which are stressed on the final vowel, and when this happens this vowel always carries a written accent (`): città, gioventù. Occasionally, the stress falls on the third- or fourth-last syllable, and these just have to be learnt by experience: camera, sedici, fotografico, piacciono, zucchero. Throughout this book, if the stress occurs on the third or fourth to last syllable, the stressed vowel is shown in italic type, as here, or in bold italic type where necessary.

2 Despite the stress falling on one syllable, all the syllables in Italian are clearly sounded. Vowels are not slurred or drawled as sometimes happens in English, and each keeps its own pure sound, which is more akin to the accent of Scotland than to southern English.

3 Consonants are more or less the same as English ones, except that the *r* is always rolled (see overleaf).

Italian pronunciation

Vowel sounds

Practise saying these words

a	like *a* in *path*	s**a**la	gr**a**zie
e	has two sounds:		
	(i) like *ai* in *pain*	c**e**ntro	v**e**la
	(ii) like *e* in *pen*	**e**cco	b**e**llo
i	like *i* in *machine*	l**i**tro	val**i**gia
o	has two sounds:		
	(i) like *o* in *note*	s**o**no	s**o**le
	(ii) like *o* in *not*	n**o**	**o**cchio
u	like *oo* in *fool*	**u**no	com**u**ne

Consonants

c	has two sounds:		
	(i) before *i* or *e* like *ch* in *cheap*	vi**c**ino	**c**entro
	(ii) otherwise like *c* in *cupboard*	**c**omprare	**c**aldo
g	has two sounds:		
	(i) before *i* or *e* like *g* in *general*	**g**iornale	**g**enerale
	(ii) otherwise like *g* in *god*	pre**g**o	do**g**ana
h	is never pronounced	**h**a	**h**anno
n	as English except when followed by a hard *c*, *g*, or a *q*, in which case it sounds like *n* in *coming*	ba**n**ca	i**n**glese
r	or **rr** is always rolled	buonase**r**a	bo**r**setta
s	has two sounds:		
	(i) like *s* in *simple*	**s**era	pa**s**ta
	(ii) like *s* in *pies* (usually between vowels)	ingle**s**e	**s**cusi

z	has two sounds:		
	(i) like *ts* in *hits*	stazione	gra*z*ie
	(ii) like *ds* in *cads*	pranzo	benzina

Double consonants are pronounced as longer versions of single ones:

cassa   autocarro

The following combinations of consonants need special attention:

ch	before *i* and **e** is pronoun-ced as *k*	**ch**iamo	**ch**e
gh	before *i* and *e* is pronoun-ced as hard *g*	alber**gh**i	tra**gh**etto
gl	before *i* sounds like *lli* in *million*	m*o*glie	bi**gl**ietto
gn	like *ni* in *onion*	si**gn**ora	ba**gn**o
sc	before *i* and *e* is pronoun-ced as *sh*	**sc**iare	a**sc**ensore
	Otherwise like *sk*	**sc**ozzese	pe**sc**are

Introduction to Italian Grammar

1 Nouns

All nouns in Italian are said to be either masculine or feminine. Most nouns ending in **-o** are masculine and most nouns ending in **-a** are feminine. But there are other endings as well, such as **-e,** and it is not always possible to tell from the ending of a word whether it is masculine or feminine, so you should always learn each new word with its gender. In the plural, nouns ending in **-o** change to **-i** and nouns ending in **-a** change to **-e.** Nouns ending in **-e** in the singular usually change to **-i** in the plural.

2 The

The word for *the* takes various forms in Italian, depending on the gender of the noun which follows, and also on the first letter of the following word.

Before masculine nouns these forms are as follows:

	Singular	*Plural*
(*a*)	**il** passaporto (*passport*)	**i** passaporti
(*b*)	**lo** spettacolo (*show*)	**gli** spettacoli
	lo zucchero (*sugar*)	
(*c*)	**l'**autocarro (*lorry*)	**gli** autocarri

You can learn these forms by remembering the following rules:
(*a*) **il**, plural **i**, is used before a masculine noun beginning with a consonant other than **s** + *consonant* or **z**.
(*b*) **lo**, plural **gli**, is used before a masculine noun beginning with **s** + *consonant* or **z**.
(*c*) **l'**, plural **gli**, is used before a masculine noun beginning with a vowel.

The word for *the* has only one form in the feminine, **la**, which is shortened to **l'** before a vowel in the singular; **le** is the plural form.

la donna (*woman*)	**le** donne (*women*)
l' arancia (*orange*)	**le** arance (*oranges*)

3 A, an

The word for *a* in Italian is **un** or **uno** before a masculine noun and **un'** or **una** before a feminine noun.

Masculine	*Feminine*
un veicolo (*vehicle*)	**un'** ora (*hour*)
uno spettacolo	
(*performance*)	**una** macchina (*car*)

As a general rule use **un** with a masculine noun unless the first consonant of the following noun is an **s** + *consonant* or **z**.

With feminine nouns, use **una** unless the first letter of the following noun is a vowel.

4 Adjectives

In Italian the ending of the adjective depends on whether the noun it accompanies is masculine or feminine. Some adjectives take **-o** as the masculine ending and **-a** as the feminine ending (e.g. **piccolo, piccola**), which become **-i** and **-e** respectively in the plural. Others end in **-e** in the singular in both masculine and feminine (e.g. **grande, inglese**) and in the plural these change to **-i**. There are many other forms to learn as you come across them. Here are some examples of nouns and adjectives from the book:

una camera doppia (*a double room*)
una camicia bianca (*a white shirt*)
Ha giornali inglesi? (*Do you have English newspapers?*)
Parcheggio custodito (*Supervised parking*)

Most adjectives come *after* the noun, but some short, everyday ones are placed *before* the noun. Again, here are some from the book:

Buona sera (*Good evening*)
i **grandi** magazzini (*department store*)
una **piccola** bottiglia (*a small bottle*)

5 This and that

The word for *this* is **questo** and the word for *that* is **quello.** These demonstrative adjectives follow the usual rules for agreement of adjectives, and **quello** changes its form considerably depending on the noun which follows. Here is the full table, together with the articles they replace:

il	i	lo	gli	la	le	l'
questo	questi	questo	questi	questa	queste	quest'
quello	quelli	quello	quegli	quella	quelle	quell'

Examples from the book include:
questa valigia *this suitcase*
Mi piace **questa** camicia *I like this shirt*

6 My, your, etc.

Although the use of possessive adjectives in this book is limited to *my* and *your*, the full list may be found useful:

Masculine		*Feminine*		
Singular	*Plural*	*Singular*	*Plural*	
il mio	i miei	la mia	le mie	*my, mine*
il tuo	i tuoi	la tua	le tue	*your, yours* (familiar)
il suo	i suoi	la sua	le sue	*his, her, its, your, yours* (formal)
il nostro	i nostri	la nostra	le nostre	*our, ours*
il vostro	i vostri	la vostra	le vostre	*your, yours* (familiar)
il loro	i loro	la loro	le loro	*their, theirs, your, yours* (formal)

As you can see, each word has four forms, masculine singular and plural and feminine singular and plural. It is important to remember that in Italian the article *the* is used with the possessive adjective except when talking about a close relative. Here are some examples from the book:

    il suo passaporto (*your passport*)

    Ho perso **la mia** chiave (*I have lost my key*)

but **Mia** moglie (*My wife*)

Also very important is the fact that possessive adjectives agree with the noun they accompany and *not* the person to whom the thing belongs.

7 I, you, etc.

The personal pronouns are not generally used in Italian except for emphasis and in certain other circumstances. This is because, unlike English, the endings of the verb change for each person, thus making it clear, usually, who the subject is. Here for the record is the complete list:

	singular			*plural*
io	*I*		noi	*we*
tu	*you* (familiar)		voi	*you* (familiar)
lui, lei	*he, she*		loro	*they*
lei	*you* (formal)		loro	*you* (formal)

Note there are three ways of saying *You* in Italian. In this book the **Lei** form is used throughout as being the correct form for the stranger or visitor to Italy. You will see that it takes the same form of the verb as *he* or *she* – the third person.

8 Prepositions (To, of, by, in, from, etc.)

There are a large number of prepositions in Italian, some of which occur in this book.

A mean *to* or *at*:

Andiamo **a** Milano. *We are going to Milan.*

When **a** is followed by a definite article (e.g. **la**) it changes its form.

Andiamo **alla** spiaggia. *We are going to the beach.*

As we can see, its form depends on the gender and number of the noun which follows:

All'ombra *In the shade*

All'hotel Victoria, per favore. *To Victoria Hotel, please.*

A also has some other meanings and uses:

Parto **alle** sette. *I leave at seven o'clock.*

Spaghetti **alla** bolognese. . . . *in the manner of Bologna.*

Una camicia **a** maniche lunghe. *A long-sleeved shirt.*

Di means *of*:

Un chilo **di** pasta. *A kilo of pasta.*

Una bottiglia **di** vino. *A bottle of wine.*

Like **a**, when **di** is followed by a definite article, its form changes according to the gender and number of the noun which follows:

Il furto **della** macchina. *The theft of the car.*

Di can also be used to mean *some* or *any*.

Ha **degli** spiccioli? *Have you any change?*

Other prepositions used in this book include:

da   *by, from*
in   *in, into*
con *with* (does not change)
per *for* (does not change)

The following table shows how all the above words change when they occur together with the article:

	il	i	lo	gli	la	le	l'
a	al	ai	allo	agli	alla	alle	all'
in	nel	nei	nello	negli	nella	nelle	nell'
da	dal	dai	dallo	dagli	dalla	dalle	dall'
di	del	dei	dello	degli	della	delle	dell'

9 Verbs

(a) All regular Italian verbs fall into one of three categories, whose infinitive endings (in English 'to do, to speak, etc,) are either **-are, -ere,** or **-ire.**

parlare (*to speak*)	**chiudere** (*to shut*)	**aprire** (*to open*)
parlo *I speak*	chiudo *I shut*	apro *I open*
parli *you speak*	chiudi *you shut*	apri *you open*
parla *he, she speaks you speak*	chiude *he, she shuts you shut*	apre *he, she opens you open*
parliamo *we speak*	chiudiamo *we shut*	apriamo *we open*
parlate *you speak*	chiudete *you shut*	aprite *you open*
parlano *they speak you speak*	chiudono *they shut you shut*	aprono *they open you open*

(b) As well as the regular verbs, which follow the pattern above, there are a large number of verbs which have a slightly different pattern. Here are some of the most common, together with some examples of their use from the book:

avere
(*to have*):
ho, hai, ha, abbiamo, avete, hanno
Ha qualcosa da dichiarare? *Do you have anything to declare?*
Ha una camera líbera? *Do you have a room vacant?*

essere
(*to be*):
sono, sei, e, siamo, siete, sono
Dov'è la via Veneto? *Where is Via Veneto?*
Sono la signora Marshall. *I am Mrs Marshall.*
È un rapido? *Is it an express train?*
È l' una. *It's one o'clock*
Sono le sette. *It's seven o'clock.*

fare
(*to do, make*):
faccio, fai, fa, facciamo, fate, fanno
Fa freddo. *It is cold weather.*
Mi faccia il pieno, per favore. *Fill up the tank, please.*

andare
(*to go*):
vado, vai, va, andiamo, andate, vanno
Andiamo a Milano. *We are going to Milan.*
Vada sempre diritto. *Go straight ahead.*

volere
(*to want*):
voglio, vuoi, vuole, vogliamo, volete, vogliono

piacere
(to please): This is the verb one uses to say one likes something or someone. To say 'I like cheese' one has to turn it round and say 'Cheese pleases me'. In Italian this would be **Mi piace il formaggio.** When the things one likes are plural 'I like beans' becomes **Mi piacciono i fagioli.** So learn **Mi piace . . .** and **Mi piacciono.**

(c) *Asking questions and saying No*
Note the following word order:
È inglese? *Are you English?*
Sì, sono inglese. *Yes, I am English.*
No, **non** sono inglese. *No, I'm not English.*
Here is a list of the more common question words:
Che? *What?* Che ore sono? *What time is it?*
Come? *How?* or *What*? Come si chiama? *What's your name? What's it called?*
Dove? *Where?* Dov'è la via Manzini? *Where is Manzini street?* Dove sono? *Where are they*?
Chi? *Who?*
Quanto? *How much?* Quanto costa? *How much is it?* Quanto costano? *How much are they?*
Note the following expressions, containing a word for *nothing*.
Non ho **nulla** da dichiarare. *I have nothing to declare.*
Non c'è **niente** di grave. *It's nothing serious.*

1 General Expressions

a. Yes, No **b.** Hello, Goodbye **c.** Please, Thank you **d.** Mr, Mrs **e.** The, This **f.** I, My . . .

Buon giorno, Signorina.

a.	**sì**	*yes*
	no	*no*

Sì, signore.	*Yes. (to a man)*
No, signora.	*No. (to a lady)*

b.	**buongiorno**	*good morning, hello*
	buona sera	*good evening*
	arrivederla, arrivederci	*goodbye*
	ciao	*hello/goodbye*

Buongiorno, signore.	*Good morning. (to a man)*
Buongiorno, Signora Rossi.	*Good morning, Mrs Rossi.*
Come sta?	*How are you?*
Molto bene, e lei?	*Very well, and you?*
Non c'è male.	*Not too bad.*
Arrivederci, signora.	*Goodbye. (to a lady)*

c.	**grazie**	*thank you*
	prego	*don't mention it*
	per favore	*please*
	scusi	*excuse me*

Grazie, signorina.	*Thank you. (to a young lady)*
Mille grazie.	*Thank you very much.*
Molto gentile.	*Very kind of you.*
Il passaporto, per favore.	*Your passport, please.*
Scusi, signora.	*Excuse me. (to a lady)*

d.

l'	**uomo**	*man*
la	**donna**	*woman, lady*
il	**bambino**	*child*
il	**ragazzo**, la **ragazza**	*boy, girl*
	Signor(e)	*Mr (in address, before a name)*
	Signora	*Mrs (in address, before a name)*
	Signorina	*Miss*

Signor Rossi.	*Mr Rossi.*
Signora Ponti.	*Mrs Ponti.*
Sono la signora Marshall.	*I am Mrs Marshall.*

e.

il (l'[1], lo[2]) (*m.*), **la (l'[1])** (*f.*)	*the (singular)*
l (gli[1, 2]) (*m.*), **le** (*f.*)	*the (plural)*
un (*m.*), **una, (un'[1])** (*f.*)	*a, an*
questo (*m.*), **questa** (*f.*)	*this*
c' è	*it/that is, there is*
ci sono	*there are*
ecco	*here is, here are*

il giorno/i giorni	*day/days*
la val*i*gia	*suitcase*
le val*i*gie	*suitcases*
questa val*i*gia	*this suitcase*
Ecco la chiave.	*Here is the key.*

f.

il	**mio** / la **mia**	*my (m.)./my (f.)*
il	**suo** / la **sua**	*your (formal m., f.)*

Il suo nome, per favore.	*Your name, please.*
La sua chiave.	*Your key*
È la mia val*i*gia.	*It is my suitcase.*
Non è la mia val*i*gia.	*It is not my suitcase.*
Mia m*o*glie.	*This is my wife.*
Mio marito.	*This is my husband.*

---

[1] Before nouns that begin with a vowel: l'acqua minerale.
[2] Before nouns that begin with s + consonant: lo spett*a*colo.

1 General Expressions

1 How do you say *good morning* to a man?

2 You want to say *good evening* to a lady. What do you say?

3 A man asks you: **Come sta?** What do you answer?

4 You want to say *goodbye* to a man. What do you say?

5 You want to say *goodbye* to your friend Luigi. What do you say?

6 You are Mrs Marshall. Someone asks you: **Il suo nome, per favore** What do you answer?

7 The policeman wants to see your passport. What does he say?

8 The customs officer asks you: **È la sua valigia?** Ask him if he means this suitcase.

9 If the suitcase belongs to you, what do you answer?

10 If the suitcase does not belong to you, what do you answer?

11 You want to apologise to a lady. What do you say?

12 You want to thank a gentleman. What do you say?

13 Mr Marshall would like to introduce his wife. What does he say?

- In Italy, you usually address a man as **signore,** a married woman as **signora** and an unmarried woman or girl as **signorina**.
  Buongiorno, signore.
  Buongiorno, signor Conti. (Note the final *e* is omitted when followed by the surname)
  Buongiorno, signora Manzoni.
  Grazie, signorina.
  However, courtesy also demands the use of qualifications and titles:
  Buongiorno, dottore. (graduate or doctor)
  Buona sera, ingegnere. (engineer)
  Grazie, professore. (university lecturer or school teacher)
  In the feminine, **dottore** becomes **dottoressa** and **professore** becomes **professoressa.**

- When being introduced to each other, Italians shake hands and say **Piacere**.

- Always use the **Lei** form of the verb when meeting someone for the first time or talking to someone you don't know well. It is used with the third person of the verb (see Grammar section)

- When saying goodbye use **Ciao** with someone you know well and otherwise the more formal **Arrivederla.**

- **Some useful words and expressions**

It is . . .	**È . . .**
It is not . . .	**Non è . . .**
good/bad	**buono/male**
better/worse	**meglio/peggio**
big/small	**grande/piccolo**
easy/difficult	**facile/difficile**
old/new	**vecchio/nuovo**
far/near	**lontano/vicino**
free/occupied	**libero/occupato**
open/closed	**aperto/chiuso**
beautiful/ugly	**bello/brutto**
too (much)	**troppo**
cheap/expensive	**a buon mercato/caro**
more/less	**più/meno**
a lot/a little	**molto/poco**
very	**molto**
It is OK.	**Va bene**

2 Arriving in Italy

a. Customs **b.** Documents **c.** Nationality

a.
la	**dogana**	*customs*
	dichiarare	*to declare*
il	**bagaglio**	*luggage*
il	**portabagagli**	*boot (of a car)*
la	**borsetta**	*handbag*
la	**valigia**	*suitcase*

Oggetti da dichiarare.	*Goods to declare.*
Nulla da dichiarare.	*Nothing to declare.*
Ha qualcosa da dichiarare?	*Anything to declare?*
No signore.	*No.*
Apra la valigia per favore	*Open your suitcase, please.*
Va bene!	*Open the boot of your car.*
Apra il portabagagli.	*Open the boot of your car.*
Va bene!	*O.K.!*
Buon viaggio!	*Have a pleasant trip!*

b.

il	**passaporto**	*passport*
la	**patente**	*driving licence*
il	**libretto di circolazione**	*car registration papers*
il	**nome**	*name, first name*
il	**cognome**	*surname*
il	**domicílio**	*place of residence*
la	**firma**	*signature*

Controllo passaporti.	*Passport control.*
Il passaporto, per favore.	*Your passport, please.*
Il suo nome?	*Your name?*
Mi chiamo . . .	*My name is . . .*

c.

la	**nazionalità**	*nationality*
l'	**Italia**	*Italy*
	italiano	*Italian*
	americano, americana	*American*
la	**Gran Bretagna**	*Great Britain*
l'	**Inghilterra**	*England*
	inglese	*English*
gli	**inglesi**	*the English*
la	**Scozia**	*Scotland*
	scozzese	*Scottish*
il	**Galles**	*Wales*
	gallese	*Welsh*
l'	**Australia**	*Australia*
	australiano	*Australian*
il	**Canada**	*Canada*
	canadese	*Canadian*
l'	**ambasciata**	*Embassy*
il	**consolato**	*consulate*

È inglese?	*Are you English?*
Sì, sono inglese.	*Yes, I am English.*
Non capisco.	*I don't understand.*
Parla inglese?	*Do you speak English?*
Ha giornali inglesi?	*Do you have English newspapers?*
Una rivista in inglese, per favore.	*A magazine in English, please.*
Come si chiama questo in italiano?	*How do you say this in Italian?*

2 Arriving in Italy

What are these called in Italian?

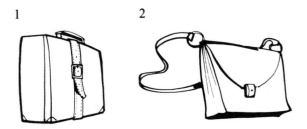

1   2

3 The customs officer asks you: **Ha qualcosa da dichiarare?** You have nothing to declare. What do you say?

4 The customs officer wants you to open the boot of your car. What does he say?

5 The customs officer wants you open your suitcase. What does he say?

6 The policeman asks you: **È inglese?** If you are English, what do you reply?

7 The policeman asks you your name. What do you say?

8 The policeman wants to see your driving licence. What does he say?

9 The policeman is satisfied and wishes you a pleasant trip. What does he say?

10 You haven't understood something in Italian. What do you say?

11 You want to know if he speaks English. How do you ask?

What are these countries called in Italian?

12 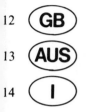 GB

13 AUS

14 I

15 You want to buy an English magazine. How do you ask the shopkeeper whether he has any?

- The address of the **British Embassy** in Rome is Via XX Settembre 80/A. Here are the addresses of some other embassies:
  Eire: Via del Pozzetto 105
  United States: Via Veneto 119/A.

- There are **British Consulates** in almost every big city. Consult the Telephone Directory under *'Consolato Britannico'*.

- British nationals need a passport to enter Italy and they are asked to register with the Police within three days of entry. Usually, if you are staying in a hotel, the manager will ask you for proof of identity and will do the registering himself.

- In Rome there is a special Police information service to assist tourists. Interpreters are available.

3 Driving a Car

a. Vehicles **b.** Roads **c.** Service Stations
d. Parking

a.	il	**veicolo**	*vehicle*
	la	**macchina**	*car*
	la	**roulotte**	*caravan*
	l'	**autocarro**	*lorry*
		andare	*to go, to drive*
	la	**velocità**	*speed*
		rallentare	*to slow down*

Veicoli lenti.	*Slow vehicles*
Veicoli veloci.	*Fast vehicles*
Autonoleggio.	*Car Rental.*
Andiamo a Milano.	*We are driving to Milan.*

b.

l'	**autostrada**	*motorway*
il	**pedaggio**	*toll*
l'	**area di servizio**	*service area*
	Uscita	*Exit*
la	**strada statale (ss)**	*Main road*
	Attenzione	*Caution!*
	Caduta massi	*Rockfall*
	Deviazione	*Diversion*
	Senso unico	*One-way street*
la	**galleria**	*tunnel*

L'autostrada a pedaggio.	*Toll motorway.*
Pagamento pedaggio.	*Toll booth.*
La strada per Firenze.	*The road to Florence.*
Accendere i fari.	*Turn your headlights on.*

c.

la	**stazione di servizio**	*service station*
la	**benzina**	*petrol*
il	**gasolio**	*diesel*
l'	**olio**	*oil*
le	**gomme**	*tyres*

Benzina normale.	*2-star petrol.*
Super.	*4-star petrol.*
Quanto?	*How much?*
Venti litri di super.	*20 litres of 4-star.*
Trentamila di super.	*30 000 lira's worth of 4-star.*
Mi faccia il pieno.	*Fill it up.*
Controlli l'olio, per favore.	*Check the oil please.*

d.

il	**parcheggio**	*parking*
il	**disco orario**	*parking disc*
il	**garage**	*garage*

Parcheggio custodito.	*(Supervised) car-park.*
Parcheggio a pagamento.	*Meter parking.*
Ha un garage?	*Do you have a garage?*

Breakdowns, Accidents → 20

3 Driving a Car

What are these called in Italian?

3 You want to rent a car. What sign do you look for?
4 The attendant wants to know how much petrol you
    want. What does he ask you?
5 You want 20 litres of 4-star. How do you ask for it?
6 You want the tank filled up. What do you say?
7 How do you ask the attendant to check the oil and
    the tyres?
8 Where does the scene in this picture take place?

Explain in Italian what the following traffic signs mean:

- **British driving licence** is valid in Italy but should be accompanied by an authorised translation, freely available from CIT (50 Conduit St, London, W1), ACI (Italian Automobile Club) and the Italian State Tourist Office (1 Princes St, London W1). Adequate motor insurance is essential and you are advised to obtain an International Green Card from your insurance company. Visitors must also carry their Vehicle Registration Book (log book).

- The Italian Government issues special reductions on the price of supergrade petrol and on motorway tolls for GB registered vehicles. Special **petrol coupons** and **motorway vouchers** are available from the AA and RAC offices and from CIT (address above). They can also be obtained at the Italian frontier from the ACI office. Petrol coupons and motorway vouchers are issued with a **Fuel card** (*Carta Carburante*) with which one can take advantage of the free breakdown service provided by the ACI to foreign tourists.

- There are two grades of petrol: *normale* = 2-star, *super* = 4-star. The carrying of petrol in a can in a vehicle is forbidden in Italy.

- The following **speed limits** are in force for motor vehicles (in km/h):

	up to 600 cc	up to 900 cc	up to 1300 cc	over 1300 cc
Towns and villages	50	50	50	50
Roads	80	90	100	110
Motorways	90	110	130	140

The 50 km/h speed limit in built-up areas in strictly enforced. You will see the 50 when you reach the outskirts of a town or village.

Drivers must give priority to all vehicles coming from the right. They must stop at a 'Give way' sign (white triangle with red border pointing down) or at a 'Stop' sign. It is compulsory for all vehicles on Italian roads to be fitted with a rear view mirror on the left-hand external side.

4 Finding Your Way

a. Maps **b.** In Town **c.** Streets **d.** Directions

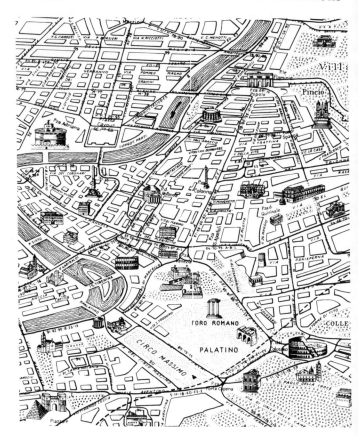

a.	la **carta**	*map*
	la **pianta della città**	*city map*

Una carta stradale, per favore.	*A road map, please.*
Una pianta di Milano, per favore.	*A street plan of Milan, please.*

b.
la	**città**	*city, town*
il	**comune**	*town hall; borough*
la	**casa**	*house*

La città di Milano.	*The city of Milan.*
Il comune di Milano.	*The municipality of Milan.*
Centro città.	*Town centre*
Il giro della città.	*Sightseeing tour of the city.*

c.
la	**via**, la **strada**	*street*
il	**viale**	*tree-lined avenue*
il	**corso**	*avenue*
la	**piazza**	*square*
il	**piazzale**	*square (with grass, trees)*
il	**ponte**	*bridge*
il	**semaforo**	*traffic light*
	Alt	*Stop (wait)*
	Avanti	*Go (pedestrians)*

Piazza San Marco.	*St. Mark's Square*
Dove abita?	*Where do you live?*
Abito in via Piave.	*I live in Via Piave.*

d.
la	**direzione**	*direction*
	dov'è?	*where is?*
la	**curva**	*bend*
	a destra	*to the right*
	a sinistra	*to the left*
	diritto	*straight ahead*
il	**nord,** il **sud**	*north, south*
l'	**est,** l' **ovest**	*east, west*

Scusi, per Pisa?	*Excuse me, which way to Pisa?*
Dov'è la via Veneto?	*Where is the Via Veneto?*
Giri a destra.	*Turn right.*
Vada sempre diritto.	*Go straight ahead.*
La prima strada a sinistra.	*The first street on the left.*
È ancora lontano?	*Is it much further?*
No, è vicino.	*No, it's nearby.*

Weights and Measures → 7, Places of Interest → 15, Excursions → 16

4 Finding Your Way

1 What does each letter
    stand for in Italian?

2 You want to buy a street map of Pisa. What do you
   say?
3 You want to buy a road map. What do you say?
4 Which word lights up on a sign when you may cross
   the street?
5 Which word lights up when you must wait?
6 Ask someone where the Via Manzini is.
7 How do you tell someone to turn right?
8 How do you tell someone to turn left?
9 You are on the motorway and you want to go to
   Foggia. You see this sign. In which direction must
   you turn?

(A2) NAPOLI	↑
(A17) AVELLINO BENEVENTO FOGGIA BARI	↗

10 Someone tells you to go straight ahead. What does he say?

11 You want to know if it's far? How do you ask?

12 Someone tells you it's the first street on the right. What does he say?

13 You are entering Milan and want to go to the city centre. Which sign must you look for?

14 Read the names of these Italian cities. Try to pronounce them as clearly as possible so that you will be understood.
Roma, Milano, Napoli, Torino, Genova, Palermo, Firenze, Bologna, Catania, Venezia.

– **Maps**, brochures, lists of hotels and prices can be obtained from the local tourist office (**Ufficio turistico**, **Azienda autonoma di soggiorno**, **Pro loco**) which are in most main tourist resorts.

– There are the following different **categories of road**:
Autostrada (Motorway – the most well known is the *Autostrada del Sole*, linking the north to the south)
Map symbol = A.
Strada Statale (Main road) Map symbol = SS
Strada Provinciale (B road)

– Useful **road signs** are:
Sosta vietata = No parking
Senso vietato = No entry
Passaggio a livello = Level crossing
Incrocio = Crossroads
Lavori in corso = Road Works ahead
Rallentare = Slow down
Svolta = Bend

– Note that although **strada** means 'street' it is never used with names of streets. Use **Via** instead.

5 Public Transport

a. Railways **b.** Aeroplanes **c.** Ships **d.** Urban Transport **e.** Information

a.

le	**ferrovie dello Stato (FS)**	*national railways*
la	**stazione**	*railway station*
il	**binario**	*track, platform*
il	**treno**	*train*
il	**rapido**	*express train*
l'	**espresso**	*fast train*
il	**treno diretto**	*direct train*
il	**treno locale**	*local train*
la	**carrozza ristorante**	*dining car*
la	**carrozza letto**	*sleeping car*
la	**carrozza cuccette**	*couchette*

La stazione centrale.	*Main station.*
Da che binario parte?	*What platform does it leave from?*
Binario 3	*Platform 3.*
È un rapido?	*Is it an express?*

b.

l'	**aeroporto**	*airport*
l'	**aereo**	*aeroplane*
il	**volo**	*flight*

Partenze internazionali.	*International departures.*
Controllo sicurezza.	*Security control.*
Consegna bagagli.	*Baggage collection.*
La tassa d'imbarco.	*Airport tax.*

c.

il	**porto**	*port*
l'	**imbarco**	*embarkment area*
la	**nave**	*ship*
il	**traghetto**	*ferry*
l'	**aliscafo**	*hydrofoil*
il	**ponte**	*deck*

d.

il	**pullman**, la **corriera**	*coach*
l'	*au***tobus**	*bus*
la	**fermata**	*stop*
il	**tassi**	*taxi*

Mi chiami un tassi.	*Call me a taxi.*
Alla stazione, per favore.	*To the station, please.*
All' hotel Victoria, per favore.	*To the Hotel Victoria, please.*
Fermi qui!	*Stop here!*

e.

	Informazioni	*Information*
l'	**orario**	*timetable*
	Partenze	*Departures*
	Arrivi	*Arrivals*
la	**destinazione**	*destination*
la	**provenienza**	*origin*
il	**ritardo**	*delay*
la	**biglietteria**	*ticket counter*
il	**biglietto**	*ticket*
il	**supplemento**	*surcharge*
la	**riduzione**	*discount*
la	**prenotazione**	*reservation*
il	**posto**	*seat*

Un biglietto per Roma.	*A ticket to Rome.*
A Venezia andata e ritorno.	*Return ticket to Venice.*
Prima (seconda) classe.	*First (second) class.*

Customs → 2, Times → 8, Money → 9

5 Public Transport

Which sign do you look for at the airport:

1 When you want information?
2 When you want to travel abroad?
3 When you want to pick up your luggage after landing?
4 When you are looking for the arrivals section?
5 What do you call a ship which you can take, for example, from Italy to Greece?
6 What do you call the kind of boat in the picture below?

Look at this railway ticket.

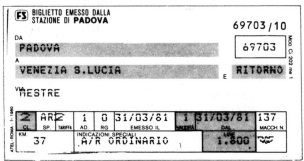

7 Where did the passenger leave from?
8 Where did the passenger go?
9 Is this a one-way or a return ticket?
10 Ask for this ticket at the ticket counter.
11 Ask what platform the train leaves from.
12 Ask if it's an express or a fast train.

13   Tell the taxi driver that you want to go to the Hotel Victoria.

14   Tell the taxi driver to stop here.

– There are five categories of **trains** in Italy:

Super-Rapido:	These run between major Italian cities. First class only. Reservation is compulsory and a supplement is charged on the price of the ticket. These trains have names such as *Settebello* and *Ambrosiano* (Milan to Rome), *Vesuvio* (Milan to Naples). *Adriatico* (Milan to Bari).
Rapido:	These are fast trains which run between large towns. Reservation compulsory and supplement payable. Some are first class only.
Espresso:	Long-distance express trains. Both classes.
Diretto:	Trains stopping at most stations. Both classes.
Locale:	Trains which stop at all stations. Both classes.

– Fares are paid on a mileage basis. Children under 4 travel free. Children between the ages of 4 and 12 enjoy a 50 % reduction. For tourists who reside outside Italy and who wish to travel extensively on Italian Railways, it is possible to obtain an unlimited travel ticket (**Biglietto turistico libera circolazione**). In Italy these are available at some main stations and in U.K. at recognised agencies. Children under 12 qualify for a reduced rate. It is also possible to obtain a **Chilometrico** ticket, valid for 3,000 kilometres, which can be used by up to five people at the same time.

– **Buses** within towns operate on a flat fare system. The method of buying tickets varies from town to town. (For example, in Rome you pay the conductor but in Milan you have to buy a book of tickets in advance from a newsagent.)

– There are **underground trains** (*Metropolitana*) in Rome and Milan.

6 Accommodation

a. Hotels, Camping   **b.** Hotel Rooms
c. Prices   **d.** Toilets

a.	l'	**hotel**	*hotel*
	l'	**albergo**	*inn, hotel*
	il	**motel**	*motel*
	la	**pensione**	*guest-house*
	il	**campeggio**	*campsite*
	l'	**ostello della gioventù**	*youth hostel*

C'è un hotel qui vicino?	*Is there a hotel near here?*
– un buon hotel.	*– a good hotel.*
Dov'è il campeggio?	*Where is the campsite?*

b.	la	**camera**	*room*
	il	**letto**	*bed*

la	**doccia**	*shower*
il	**bagno**	*bath*
la	**chiave**	*key*
il	**pianterreno (T)**	*ground floor*
il	**piano**	*floor*
la	**scala**	*stairs*
l'	**ascensore**	*lift*

Ha una camera libera?	*Do you have a room vacant?*
– per una notte.	*– for one night.*
– per due settimane	*– for two weeks*
Ho prenotato una camera.	*I have booked a room.*
Una camera singola.	*A single room.*
Una doppia.	*A double room.*
Il letto matrimoniale.	*Double bed.*
Una camera a due letti.	*A twin-bed room.*
Una camera con bagno.	*A room with bath.*
La prendo.	*I'll take it.*
Per favore, la chiave.	*The key, please.*
Il numero della camera.	*The room number.*
La doccia non funziona.	*The shower doesn't work.*
È tutto occupato.	*Sorry, it's full.*

c.

il	**prezzo**	*price*
	caro	*expensive*
il	**conto**	*bill*
la	**mezza pensione**	*half board*
la	**pensione completa**	*full board*

Quanto costa la camera?	*How much is the room?*
È (troppo) cara.	*It's (too) expensive.*
Mi faccia il conto, per favore.	*I want the bill, please.*
Ecco il conto, signore.	*Here is your bill, sir.*

d.

il	**gabinetto, la toilette**	*toilet*
	Signori/Signore	*Gentlemen/Ladies*
	occupato	*occupied*
	libero	*vacant*

Customs → 2, Parking → 3, Money → 9, Meals → 10

6 Accommodation

What are these called in Italian?

1
2

3 You are looking for a hotel. How do you ask a passer-by?

4 You have arrived at the reception desk. How do you ask if they have a room free?

5 How do you say you have booked a room for one week?

6 Say you want a double room for two nights.

7 Say you want a single room with bath.

8 Say you want a twin-bedded room with shower.

9 Ask how much the room costs.

10 Say that you find that too expensive.

11 You are in the lift and want to go to the ground floor. Which button do you press?

12 Tell the desk clerk that the shower is not working.

13 You want to pay the bill. What do you say?

14 You want to know where the Youth Hostel is. How do you ask?

15 What do you see in the picture below?

- **Hotels** are divided into 5 categories: Deluxe, First, Second, Third, Fourth. *Pensioni* (guest houses) have three categories: I, II, III.
- By law Hotels and Pensioni must display their **prices** in every room of the establishment. The fixed charge, authorised by the Tourist Board, depends on the category, type of room, season and importance of the locality. Usually, the price does not include breakfast. In many tourist resorts the hotel management prefers to offer rooms only on a full-board basis.
- There are over 1600 **campsites** in Italy. A full list of the sites *(Campeggi e Villagi Turistici)* can be obtained from the Touring Club Italiano. Abridged lists can be obtained from either the Centro Internazionale Prenotazioni, Federcampeggio, Capello Postale 23, 50041 Calenzano (Firenze) Italy, or from the Italian State Tourist Office when available. It is advisable only to camp in official sites.
- If you want to stay in a **Youth Hostel**, you can obtain a full list from the Italian Youth Hostels Association (Associazione Italiana Alberghi per la Gioventù, Palazzo della Civilta del Lavoro, Quadrato della Concordia, 00144, EUR Rome).

7 Numbers, Weights and Measures

a. Numbers **b.** Weights and Measures

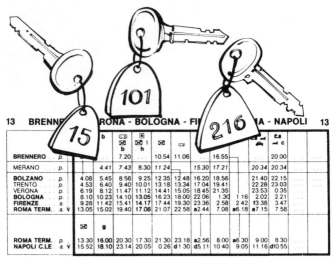

		b	h	1 h						c
BRENNERO p.			7.20		10.54	11.06		16.55		20.00
MERANO p.		4.41	7.43	8.30	11.24		15.30	17.21		20.34	20.34
BOLZANO p.	4.08	5.45	8.56	9.25	12.35	12.48	16.20	18.56		21.40	22.15
TRENTO p.	4.53	6.40	9.40	10.01	13.18	13.34	17.04	19.41		22.28	23.03
VERONA p.	6.19	8.12	11.47	11.12	14.41	15.05	18.45	21.35		23.53	0.35
BOLOGNA p.	8.10	10.23	14.10	13.05	16.23	18.00	22.06	1.30	1.16	2.02	2.21
FIRENZE a.	9.28	11.42	15.41	14.17	17.44	19.30	23.36	2.58	2.42	f3.38	3.47
ROMA TERM. a. V	13.05	15.02	19.40	17.08	21.07	22.58	a2.44	7.08	a6.18	a7.15	7.58
		g									
ROMA TERM. p.	13.30	16.00	20.30	17.30	21.30	23.18	a2.56	8.00	a6.30	9.00	8.30
NAPOLI C.LE a. V	15.52	18.10	23.14	20.05	0.26	d1.30	d5.11	10.40	9.05	11.16	d10.55

N.B. – Trasbordo a Roma.
a Roma Tiburtina. – **b** Trasbordo a Bologna – **c** ⇌ 2a cl. – **d** Napoli C.F. – **e⇌** 1a cl. – **f** Firenze C.M. – **g** Nella 1a cl. prenotazione obbligatoria. – **h** Sull'elettromotrice Roma-Bolzano prenotazione obbligatoria

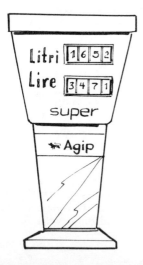

SERIE C   N. 361736

REPUBBLICA ITALIANA
MINISTERO PER I BENI CULTURALI E AMBIENTALI
UFFICIO CENTRALE PER I BENI AMBIENTALI,
ARCHITETTONICI, ARCHEOLOGICI, ARTISTICI E STORICI
BIGLIETTO D'INGRESSO
LIRE 250
(TARIFFA INTERA)
1.250

a.

0 **zero**	10 **dieci**	20 **venti**
1 **uno**	11 **undici**	21 **ventuno**
2 **due**	12 **dodici**	22 **ventidue**
3 **tre**	13 **tredici**	23 **ventitre**
4 **quattro**	14 **quattordici**	28 **ventotto**
5 **cinque**	15 **quindici**	29 **ventinove**
6 **sei**	16 **sedici**	30 **trenta**
7 **sette**	17 **diciassette**	31 **trentuno**
8 **otto**	18 **diciotto**	32 **trentadue**
9 **nove**	19 **diciannove**	33 **trentatrè**
		38 **trentotto**
		39 **trentanove**

40 **quaranta**	120 **cento venti**	1 000 **mille**
50 **cinquanta**	200 **duecento**	2 000 **duemila**
60 **sessanta**	300 **trecento**	3 000 **tremila**
70 **settanta**	400 **quattrocento**	5 000 **cinquemila**
80 **ottanta**	500 **cinquecento**	10 000 **diecimila**
90 **novanta**	600 **seicento**	20 000 **ventimila**
100 **cento**	700 **settecento**	50 000 **cinquantamila**
101 **cento uno**	800 **ottocento**	100 000 **centomila**
or **centuno**	900 **novecento**	500 000 **cinquecentomila**
		1 000 000 **un milione**

b.

il **grammo**	*gram*
un **etto**	*100 grams*
il **chilo**	*kilogram*
il **litro**	*litre*
il **metro**	*metre*
il **chilometro**	*kilometre*
il **centimetro**	*centimetre*
quanto?	*how much? how many?*
poco	*little*
molto	*much*

Due etti e mezzo di pomodori.	*250 grams of tomatoes.*
Mezzo chilo di burro.	*Half a kilo of butter.*
Cinquanta chilometri per Venezia.	*50 kilometres to Venice.*
A circa 400 metri dalla stazione centrale.	*About 400 metres from the main station.*

Times and Dates → 8

7   Numbers, Weights and Measures

In which rooms are the hotel guests staying?

1   Signor Rossi.

2   Signor Ponti.

3   Signor Marshall.

4   Signor Smith.

From which platform do these trains leave?

ORARIO		
Partenze		Binario
Genova	9.03	5
Torino	9.15	3
Trieste	9.45	6
Roma	10.00	7
Trieste	10.50	6
Verona	10.55	2

5   The train to Genoa.
6   The train to Turin.
7   The train to Trieste.
8   The train to Rome.
9   The train to Verona.

10 Read the following distances in Italian:
  (a) Brennero–Venezia   300 km
  (b) Brennero–Milano   350 km
  (c) Brennero–Firenze   460 km
  (d) Brennero–Roma   740 km
  (e) Brennero–Napoli   950 km
  (f) Brennero–Bari   1050 km

11 How many lire did the car driver pay in toll charges on the motorway?

12 You want to buy half a kilo of tomatoes. What do you say?

13 How do you ask for 250 grams of butter?

14 How do you ask for a kilo of pasta?

– Italians use the decimal system. The most common weight is the **chilo** (1000 grams or 2.2 lbs). For smaller quantities they use the **etto** (100 grams or just under 1/4 lb).
NB 1 lb = 0.45 kg; 1 pint = 0.57 litres; 1 gallon = 4.54 litres; 1 mile = 1.6 km; 8 km = 5 miles

8 Times and Dates

a. Telling the Time **b.** Times of the Day
c. Week and Month

Venezia – i Mori

a.

l'	**orologio**	*watch, clock*
l'	**ora**	*hour, time*
il	**minuto**	*minute*
il	**momento**	*moment*

Un'ora.	*One hour.*
Mezz'ora	*Half an hour.*
Un quarto d'ora	*Quarter of an hour.*
Che ore sono?	*What time is it?*
È l'una.	*It is 1 o'clock*
Sono le due.	*It is 2 o'clock.*
Sono le sei di mattina.	*It is 6 am*
Sona le sei e mezzo.	*It is half past 6.*
Sono le sei e un quarto.	*It is a quarter past 6.*
Sona le sei meno un quarto.	*It is a quarter to 6.*

Quando?	*When?*
Alle otto di sera.	*At 8 pm*
Dalle ore 6 alle ore 14.	*From 6 am to 2 pm*
Un momento, per favore!	*One moment, please!*

b.

il	**giorno**	*day*
la	**mattina, il mattino**	*morning*
il	**mezzogiorno**	*noon, midday*
il	**pomeriggio**	*afternoon*
la	**sera**	*evening*
la	**notte**	*night*
la	**mezzanotte**	*midnight*
	oggi	*today*
	ieri	*yesterday*
	(dopo)domani	*(the day after) tomorrow*
	tutti i giorni	*everyday*

Quando parte?	*When are you leaving?*
Domani mattina alle otto.	*Tomorrow morning at 8.*
Oggi è il venticinque luglio.	*Today is the 25th of July.*
A che ora parte il treno?	*When does the train leave?*
A mezzogiorno.	*At midday.*
Arriva alle sette.	*It arrives at seven.*
Quanto tempo si impiega?	*How long does it take?*

c.

la	**settimana**	*week*
	lunedì	*Monday*
	martedì	*Tuesday*
	mercoledì	*Wednesday*
	giovedì	*Thursday*
	venerdì	*Friday*
	sabato	*Saturday*
	domenica	*Sunday*
il	**mese**	*month*
l'	**anno**	*year*

Chiuso lunedì.	*Closed on Monday.*
Sabato, 30 agosto.	*Saturday, 30th August.*
La settimana prossima.	*Next week.*
La settimana scorsa.	*Last week.*

Public Transport → 5   Numbers → 7

8 Times and Dates

1 How do you say the following in Italian:
(a) one hour; (b) half an hour; (c) quarter of an hour.

2 In Italian what is:
(a) the time of day between sunrise and noon;
(b) the time of day between noon and sunset;
(c) the time of day when it is dark?

3 What are the following in Italian:
(a) one day, (b) one week; (c) one year?

4 You want to know the time. What do you say?

5 Say what the time is for each of the clocks below:

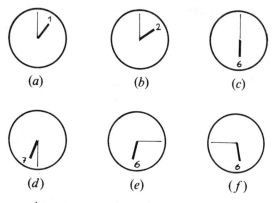

(a) (b) (c)

(d) (e) (f)

6 You arrive at a petrol station and you see the following sign:

oggi
chiuso

Can you buy petrol? (Answer **sì** or **no**.)

7   It is one o'clock. You want to go into a shop. You find the following sign on the door:

```
ORARIO

Mattino        10.00 - 12.30
Pomeriggio     16.00 - 19.30
```

Can you buy something at this time? (Answer **sì** or **no**.)

8   Someone asks when you are leaving. Say you are leaving at midnight.

9   You want to know what time the plane leaves. What do you say?

10   Someone asks when the train will arrive. Say it arrives at 7 pm.

— **Dates** are always given in cardinal numbers except for the first day of the month.

    il primo maggio   — the first of May
    il due maggio   — the second of May
    il tre maggio   — the third of May

— The **months** are as follows:

gennaio	*maggio*	*settembre*
febbraio	*giugno*	*ottobre*
marzo	*luglio*	*novembre*
aprile	*agosto*	*dicembre*

— To say 'on Monday', 'On Tuesday', etc. you simply use *lunedì*, *martedì*, etc. To say 'on Wednesdays' you can use either *ogni mercoledì* or *tutti i mercoledì*.

9 Money and Shopping

a. Money **b.** At the Bank, Changing Money
c. Shopping **d.** Paying

a.

il	**denaro,** i **soldi**	*money*
il	**biglietto**	*note*
gli	**spiccioli**	*small change*
la	**lira**	*lira*

cinquemila lire.	*5 000 lire*
diecimila lire.	*10 000 lire*
Ha degli spiccioli?	*Have you got small change?*

b.

la	**banca**	*Bank*
il	**cambio**	*change*
	cambiare	*to change*
	travellers cheque	*traveller's cheque*
la	**carta di credito**	*credit-card*

Vorrei cambiare cinquanta sterline in lire.	*I would like to change £50 into lire.*
Un biglietto da ventimila.	*A twenty-thousand lire note.*

c.

	comprare	*to buy*
il	**negozio**	*shop*
i	**grandi magazzini**	*department store*
il	**mercato**	*market*
il	**supermercato**	*supermarket*
	Entrata libera.	*No obligation to buy.*
l'	**offerta speciale**	*special offer*
l'	**orario**	*business hours*

Che cosa desidera?	*What would you like?*
Vorrei una camicia.	*I'd like a shirt.*
Ha una camicia bianca?	*Do you have a white shirt?*
Mi piace questa camicia.	*I like this shirt.*
La prendo.	*I'll take it.*
Qual cosa d' altro?	*Would you like anything else?*
Grazie, basta così.	*Thank you, that's all.*

d.

il	**prezzo**	*price*
	pagare	*to pay*
la	**cassa**	*cashier*
	caro	*expensive*
	gratuito	*free*

Quanto costa?	*How much is it?*
Quanto costano 10 000 lire.	*How much are they? 10 000 lire.*
Non è caro.	*It is not expensive.*
È (troppo) caro.	*It is (too) expensive.*

Numbers → 7, Clothing → 19

9 Money and Shopping

1 You want to change some money. What building do you look for?
2 You want to change £100 into lire. What do you say?
3 You enter a shop. What does the shop assistant ask you?
4 You want to buy a handbag (**borsetta**). What do you say?
5 You want to know if they have a white handbag. What do you say?
6 You want to know how much the handbag costs. What do you say?
7 If you like the hand bag, what do you say?

```
SUPERMERCATO
   ITALIA

-  03.560RESTO

-  10.000 *
-  06.440TOTAL

-  00.030 *
-  00.150 *
-  00.720 *
-  01.550 *
-  01.800 *
-  00.150 *
-  00.570 *
-  00.900 *
-  00.570 *

8989  30 III

  CASSA   1
TEL. 655969
  GRAZIE
```

Here is a receipt from a supermarket.

8 What is the total amount of the purchases?
9 How many lire did the customer give the cashier?
10 How much change did the cashier give the customer *(Resto)*?
11 Read aloud the prices on the receipt (from the bottom to the top).

12 The assistant asks if you want anything else. What does she say?
13 You don't want anything else, so what do you say?
14 What is a special offer called in Italian?

- In Italy **banks** are guarded by security guards. There is no need to be afraid of them. They are there for your protection.

- 'Bank' is translated as *banca* but you will often see the word *banco* in names. For example: *Banco di Roma*.

- Here is a list of names of the most common shops:
  Farmacia *Chemist*
  Panetteria *Baker*
  Macelleria *Butcher*
  Frutta e Verdura *Greengrocer*
  Rivendita di Giornali *Newsagent*
  Mercato (*Open*) *market*
  Supermercato *Supermarket*
  Salumeria *Delicatessen*
  Pescheria *Fishmonger*
  Alimentari *Groceries*
  Tabaccaio *Tobacconist*
  Negozio di Abbigliamento *Clothes shop*
  Negozio di Dischi *Record shop*
  Libreria *Bookshop*

- Shops open at 08.30/09.00 and close for lunch at 13.00 in most towns. They reopen at 15.30 or 16.00 and close at 19.30 or 20.00. There may be variations in these times depending on the season (and on agreements with the local Chamber of Commerce). Some shops, (shoes, leather goods, clothes shops, books) are closed on Saturday afternoons.

- **Chain stores** such as Upim, Standa and La Rinascente may be found in almost every town.

- **Banks** are closed on Saturdays, Sundays and Public Holidays (see Unit 16). They are open from 08.30 to 13.30 and for a short time generally between 15.00 and 16.00.

10 Meals

a. Meals   **b.** Tableware   **c.** Breakfast
d. Snacks

a.	il	**pasto**	*meal*
	la	**colazione**	*breakfast*
	il	**pranzo**	*lunch, dinner*
	la	**cena**	*dinner*
		far colazione	*to have breakfast*
		pranzare	*to have lunch*
		cenare	*to have dinner*
	la	**sala da pranzo**	*dining room*
		mangiare	*to eat*
		bere	*to drink*
b.	la	**tazza**	*cup*
	il	**bicchiere**	*glass*
	la	**bottiglia**	*bottle*

la	**caraffa**	*jug*
il	**piatto**	*plate*
il	**cucchiaio**	*spoon*
la	**forchetta**	*fork*
il	**coltello**	*knife*
il	**tovagliolo**	*napkin*

Una tazza di caffè.	*A cup of coffee.*
Un bicchiere di latte.	*A glass of milk.*
Una bottiglia di vino.	*A bottle of wine.*

c.

il	**pane**	*bread*
il	**panino**	*roll*
il	**burro**	*butter*
la	**marmellata**	*marmalade, jam*
il	**caffè**	*coffee*
il	**caffelatte**	*coffee with milk*
il	**tè**	*tea*

Caffè o tè	*Would you like coffee or tea?*
Tè al limone.	*Tea with lemon.*
La marmellata di pesche.	*Peach jam.*

d.

il	**toast**	*toast*
i	**tramezzini**	*open sandwiches*
la	**pizza**	*pizza*
il	**prosciutto**	*ham*
il	**salame**	*salami*
la	**mortadella**	*type of sausage*

Toast al prosciutto.	*Toast with ham.*
Prosciutto crudo/cotto.	*Raw ham/boiled ham.*
Pizza margherita.	*Plain pizza.*
Pizza al prosciutto.	*Pizza with ham.*
Pizza ai funghi.	*Pizza with mushrooms.*

Paying → 9, Restaurants → 11, Drinking → 14

10 Meals

1 What are the three meals of the day called in Italian?

2 What are the following called in Italian?

(e) (f) (a) (b) (c) (d)

3 What is in the cup?

4 What are these called in Italian?

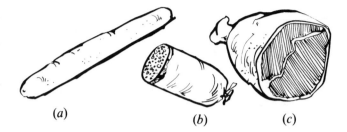

(a)   (b)   (c)

5 You'd like a glass of wine. What do you say to the waiter?

6 How would you ask for a cup of tea?

7 You want coffee with milk. What do you ask for?

8 Ask for a pizza with mushrooms.

- Traditionally the **main meal** is at lunchtime but in the big cities it is becoming more common to have a lighter lunch at work or in a nearby bar or rosticceria.
- **Breakfast** is a light meal consisting of biscuits or toast and jam with **caffè e latte.** If you go to a bar for breakfast, ask for a **cappuccino** (strong black coffee with a touch of milk). It can be accompanied by a pasta ('pastry' which has many varieties: **brioche, cannoncino, bignè alla crema,** etc.)
- The **pizza** was originally the poor man's meal for the people of Naples. It has, however, become a national dish of Italy. The dough is made of flour, yeast, oil and salt. Imagination and mastery are shown by the ingredients the cook uses: tomatoes, anchovies, ham, mushrooms, seafood, cheese, eggs, etc. The spices used are oregano and basil. Pizza is always freshly prepared and served warm.

11   Restaurants

a. Restaurants   **b.** Service, Menu
c. Seasonings   **d.** The Bill

Venezia – Basílica di San Marco

a.

il	**ristorante**	*restaurant*
la	**trattoria**	*restaurant*
il	**bar**	*bar*
il	**caffè**	*cafeteria*
la	**pasticceria**	*pastry shop*
la	**pizzeria**	*pizzeria*
la	**tavola calda**	*snack bar*
la	**tavola**, il **tavolo**	*table*
il	**posto**	*seat*
la	**terrazza**	*terrace*

| Un tavolo per due persone, per favore. | A table for two, please. |
| È libero questo posto? | Is this seat free? |

b.

il **menù**	menu
il **coperto**	cover charge
l' **antipasto**	starter, hors d'oeuvre
il **formaggio**	cheese
la **frutta**	fruit
il **gelato**	ice cream
il **dolce**	dessert

Cameriere, il menù per favore.	Waiter, the menu please.
Prendo . . .	I'll have . . .
E da bere?	What would you like to drink?
Buon appetito!	Enjoy your meal!
Il piatto del giorno.	Today's speciality.

c.

lo **zucchero**	sugar
il **sale**	salt
il **pepe**	pepper
l' **aceto**	vinegar
l' **olio**	oil

| Mi porta il sale, per favore? | Would you bring me the salt, please? |

d.

il **cameriere**	waiter
il **conto**	bill
la **ricevuta**	receipt
la **mancia**	tip

| Cameriere, il conto, per favore. | Waiter, the bill, please. |
| Questo è per Lei. | This is for you. |

Toilets → 6, Paying → 9, Meals → 10, Drinking → 14

11 Restaurants

1 Where do you go:
  (a) to have lunch or dinner?
  (b) to have a drink?
  (c) to have a cup of coffee?
  (d) to have a pizza?

2 In a restaurant how do you ask if a seat is free?

3 Tell the waiter you want a table for three.

4 Ask the waiter to bring the menu.

5 Tell the waiter you'd like today's speciality.

6 After you have ordered your meal, the waiter will ask you what you would like to drink. What does he say?

7 What is in these containers?

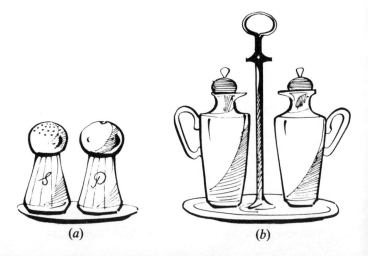

(a)   (b)

8 Attract the waiter's attention and ask him to bring you the oil and vinegar.

9 How do you ask for your bill?

10 What do you say to the waiter as you give a tip?

- **Meals** are served in the afternoon from 12.00 to 15.00 and in the evening after 20.00 (slightly earlier in Northern Italy).

- The **bar** is a place where you can have coffee and other drinks. There are no licensing hours. You can usually buy there cigarettes, stamps and a variety of sweets and postcards. Drinks are cheaper at the counter than at the table.

- Italian **restaurants** charge you for table setting (cover-charge or **coperto**).

- Restaurants are obliged to give you a receipt called **ricevuta fiscale.** Hold onto this, as it may be checked by tax officials.

- **Service charges** vary from 10 to 15 per cent, and are added to the total. If you are particularly pleased with the service you have received, you can, of course, leave an extra tip.

- In many tourist resorts the restaurants have introduced a **fixed menu. (il menu turistico)** which is cheaper but restricts choice. You can get pizzas and snacks in a pizzeria or rosticceria.

12 Pasta, Meat, Fish

a. Pasta, Soups   **b.** Meat
c. Poultry, Eggs   **d.** Fish

a.

la	**pasta**	*pasta*
gli	**spaghetti**	*spaghetti*
i	**maccheroni**	*macaroni*
i	**ravioli**	*ravioli*
i	**tortellini**	*tortellini*
il	**risotto**	*risotto*
il	**parmigiano**	*Parmesan cheese*
la	**minestra**	*vegetable soup with noodles*
la	**zuppa**	*soup*

Pasta all'uovo.	*Egg noodles.*
Pastasciutta.	*Noodles.*
Spaghetti alla bolognese.	*Spaghetti with meat sauce.*
Zuppa di verdura.	*Vegetable soup.*
Zuppa di pesce.	*Fish soup.*
Il parmigiano grattugiato.	*Grated Parmesan cheese.*

b.

la	**carne**	*meat*
il	**manzo**	*beef*
il	**vitello**	*veal*
il	**maiale**	*pork*
l'	**agnello**	*lamb*
la	**cotoletta**	*escalope*
la	**scaloppina**	*cutlet*
la	**braciola**	*grilled chop*
la	**bistecca**	*steak*
il	**fegato**	*liver*
il	**prosciutto**	*ham*
il	**sugo**	*tomato sauce*
la	**salsa**	*sauce*

Cotoletta di vitello.	*Veal escalope.*
Cotoletta alla milanese.	*Breaded veal escalope.*
Braciola di maiale.	*Grilled pork chop.*
Fegato fritto.	*Fried liver.*
La salsa di pomodoro.	*Tomato purée.*

c.

il	**pollo**	*chicken*
il	**pollo novello**	*young chicken*
l'	**uovo**	*egg*
l'	**omelette**	*omelette*

Pollo arrosto.	*Roast chicken.*
Pollo lesso.	*Boiled chicken.*
Uova al prosciutto.	*Ham and eggs.*

d.

il	**pesce**	*fish*
il	**merluzzo**	*cod*
la	**sogliola**	*sole*
il	**tonno**	*tuna*
il	**baccalà**	*dried salted cod*
	frutti di mare	*shellfish*
i	**calamari**	*squid*
i	**gamberi**	*prawns*
le	**cozze**	*mussels*

Pesce fritto.	*Fried fish.*
Filetti di merluzzo.	*Cod fillet.*
Fritto misto.	*Mixed fried fish dish.*

What is being served here?

1

2

3

4

How do you ask the waiter for the following?

5   Vegetable soup.

6   Spaghetti with meat sauce.

7   Fish soup.

8   Breaded veal escalope.

9   Fried liver.

10 Roast chicken.

11 Cod fillet.

12 Ham and eggs.

- There are more than 300 kinds of pasta in Italy: spaghetti, ravioli, cannelloni, tagliatelle, fusilli, agnolotti, farfalle, stelline, vermicelli, etc.

- Pasta is served as a first course (**primo piatto**) before meat and fish dishes.

- Two spaghetti dishes which are often served are:
  Spaghetti alla napoletana (with tomato sauce).
  Spaghetti alla bolognese (with tomato and meat sauce).

- Soups, pasta etc, are served with **Parmesan cheese** at no extra charge.

- On an Italian menu one will find the following headings:
antipasti	hors d'oeuvres (starters)
primi	first courses
secondi	second courses
contorni	vegetables
desserts	fruit or desserts

13 Vegetables, Fruit, Desserts

a. Vegetables **b.** Fruit **c.** Desserts, Sweets

a.

	Verdura	*Vegetables*
i	**contorni vari**	*mixed vegetables and salads*
le	**patate**	*potatoes*
le	**patate fritte**	*potato chips*
le	**carote**	*carrots*
gli	**asparagi**	*asparagus*
la	**cipolla**	*onion*
il	**pomodoro**	*tomato*
i	**piselli**	*peas*
i	**fagioli**	*beans*
i	**fagiolini**	*French beans*
gli	**spinaci**	*spinach*
la	**melanzana**	*aubergine*
il	**peperone**	*pepper*
l'	**insalata**	*salad*
il	**carciofo**	*artichoke*

il	**cavolfiore**	*cauliflower*
il	**finocchio**	*fennel*
l'	**oliva**	*olive*
il	**riso**	*rice*

Insalata verde.	*Green salad.*
Insalata di pomodoro.	*Tomato salad.*
Insalata russa.	*Russian salad.*
Piselli con prosciutto.	*Peas with ham.*

b.

	Frutta	*Fruit*
la	**macedonia**	*fruit salad*
la	**mela**	*apple*
l'	**arancia**	*orange*
il	**limone**	*lemon*
la	**pesca**	*peach*
le	**fragole**	*strawberries*
l'	**uva**	*grape*
il	**melone**	*melon*

Macedonia con panna.	*Fruit salad with cream.*
Melone e prosciutto.	*Melon and ham.*

c.

il	**gelato**	*ice cream*
la	**vaniglia**	*vanilla*
la	**coppa**	*bowl of ice cream*
la	**gelateria**	*ice cream parlour*
la	**torta**	*cake*
la	**crema**	*custard*
la	**panna**	*fresh cream*
i	**pasticcini**	*pastries*
i	**biscotti**	*biscuits*
la	**cioccolata**	*chocolate, cocoa*

Un gelato con panna.	*Ice cream with cream.*
Gelato alla vaniglia.	*Vanilla ice cream.*
Gelato di limone.	*Lemon ice cream.*
Gelato misto.	*Mixed ice cream.*
Torta di mele.	*Apple tart.*
Il cioccolato al latte.	*Milk chocolate.*

13 Vegetables, Fruit, Desserts

What are the following called in Italian? Say that you like them.

Start: **Mi piace/Mi piacciono . . .** *(I like . . .)*

Example: 1. I fagioli. Mi piacciono i fagioli.

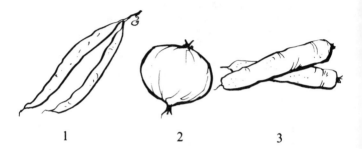

1   2   3

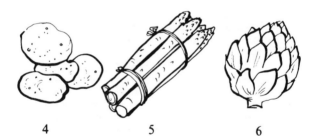

4   5   6

7   8   9

10   How do you ask for a green salad?

11   How do you ask for melon and ham?

12   How do you ask for a fruit salad with cream?

13   You want to eat some ice cream.
   (*a*) Say you want ice cream with cream.
   (*b*) Say you want a vanilla ice cream.
   (*c*) Say you want a lemon ice cream.
   (*d*) Say you want a strawberry ice cream.

– Units 12 and 13 cover the basic words needed to understand an Italian **menu**. Don't hesitate, however, to order even if you don't understand everything you read. Let yourself be surprised by the wide variety of dishes. How about visiting an Italian restaurant before you go on your holiday?

14 Drinking and Smoking

a. Non-alcoholic Beverages **b.** Alcoholic
Beverages **c.** Smoking

a.	le	**bevande**	*drinks, beverages*
	l'	**acqua minerale**	*mineral water*
	la	**limonata**	*lemonade, fresh lemon juice*
	la	**spremuta d'arancia**	*fresh orange juice*
	il	**caffè**	*coffee*
	l'	**espresso**	*espresso*
	il	**cappuccino**	*cappuccino*

il	**decaffeinato**	*decaffeinated coffee*
il	**latte**	*milk*
il	**tè**	*tea*

Acqua minerale gassata/ non gassata.	*Carbonated/non-carbonated mineral water.*
Succo di frutta.	*Fruit juice.*
Succo di mela.	*Apple juice.*
Succo di pomodoro.	*Tomato juice.*

b.

la	**birra**	*beer*
il	**vino**	*wine*
il	**vermut**	*vermouth*
il	**liquore**	*liqueur*
la	**grappa**	*strong brandy*
lo	**spumante**	*sparkling wine*
la	**bottiglia**	*bottle*
l'	**apribottiglia**	*bottle opener*
il	**cavatappi**	*corkscrew*

Vino bianco.	*White wine.*
Vino rosso.	*Red wine.*
Vino da tavola.	*House wine.*
Vino nostrano.	*Local wine.*
Una piccola bottiglia di vino rosso.	*A small bottle of red wine.*
Un quarto di vino rosso.	*A small glass of red wine (1/4 litre).*

c.

la	**sigaretta**	*cigarette*
il	**sigaro**	*cigar*
l'	**accendino**	*lighter*
i	**fiammiferi**	*matches*
il	**portacenere**	*ashtray*
	Tabaccheria	*Tobacconist*

Un pacchetto di sigarette.	*A packet of cigarettes.*
Sigarette con/senza filtro.	*Filtered/unfiltered cigarettes.*
Una scatola di fiammiferi.	*A box of matches.*
Vietato fumare.	*No smoking.*

Meals → 10

14 Drinking and Smoking

Order the following drinks at a **bar** or **caffè:**

1 A cappuccino.

2 A coffee espresso.

3 A non-carbonated mineral water.

4 A glass of tomato juice.

5 A small glass (1/4 litre) of white wine.

6 A beer.

You have ordered a meal in a restaurant. The waiter asks if you would like anything to drink. Say you would like the following items.
Start: **Vorrei . . .** (*I would like . . .*)

7 A bottle of the house wine.

8 A bottle of white wine.

9 A glass of cognac.

10 What are these called in Italian?

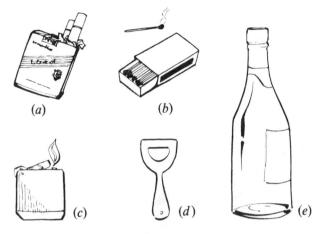

(a)   (b)

(c)   (d)   (e)

- Italy is very well-known for its red and white wines. There are such well-known wines as Chianti from Toscana, Làcrima Christi from the area around Naples, and Barolo from Lombardia.
  Every region boasts its own selection of ordinary and quality wines (**DOC** means **Denominazione di Origine Controllata**).
- Italian **sparkling wine** is sweet. Among the well-known types are Moscato, Asti Spumante and many others.
- **Tobacco** and **salt** are sold at the original price (together with stamps) in state-run stores with this symbol:

- In most restaurants and bars they now serve bottled mineral water instead of tap water. One can choose between **acqua minerale gassata** (carbonated) or **acqua minerale non gassata** (still).

15 Sightseeing and Entertainment

a. Tourism **b.** Places of Interest
c. Entertainment **d.** Admission

Roma – Basílica di San Pietro

a.

il	**turista**	*tourist*
	Azienda di soggiorno	*Tourist Information Bureau*
l'	**agenzia di viaggi**	*travel agency*
l'	**opuscolo**	*brochure*
la	**guida**	*travel guide*

Ente Nazionale Italiano per il Turismo (ENIT).	*Government Tourist Office.*
Una guida di Roma.	*A guide-book of Rome.*
Dov' è l'ufficio turistico?	*Where is the tourist office?*

b.

	edifici storici	*historical buildings*
il	**museo**	*museum*
la	**galleria**	*art gallery*
l'	**opera d'arte**	*work of art*
il	**quadro**	*painting*
la	**statua**	*statue*
l'	**affresco**	*fresco*

il	**palazzo**	*palace*
il	**castello**	*castle*
il	**ponte**	*bridge*
la	**chiesa**	*church*
la	**basilica**	*basilica*
il	**duomo**	*cathedral*
il	**campanile**	*bell tower*
la	**torre**	*tower*
la	**fontana**	*fountain*
il	**tempio**	*temple*
la	**colonna**	*pillar*
l'	**arco**	*arch*

La galleria degli Uffizi.	*The Uffizi Gallery (Florence).*
Il Cenacolo di Leonardo da Vinci.	*Leonardo da Vinci's 'Last Supper'*
Il ponte di Rialto.	*The Rialto bridge (Venice).*
Il duomo di Firenze.	*The Cathedral of Florence.*
La torre di Pisa.	*The Leaning Tower of Pisa.*

c.

l'	**opera**	*opera*
il	**teatro**	*theatre*
lo	**spettacolo**	*performance*
il	**cinema**	*cinema*
la	**partita di calcio**	*football match*

A che ora comincia lo spettacolo?	*What time does the show begin?*

d.

l'	**orario**	*opening hours*
	aperto	*open*
	chiuso	*closed*
l'	**entrata**	*entrance*
l'	**uscita**	*exit*
	spingere	*to press, to push*
	tirare	*to pull*
la	**cassa**	*ticket window*
il	**biglietto d'ingresso**	*admission ticket*
	visitare	*to visit*

A che ora apre/chiude?	*What time does it open/shut?*
La visita con guida.	*Guided tour.*
Vietato l'ingresso.	*No entry.*

Do you recognise these tourist attractions? Can you name them?

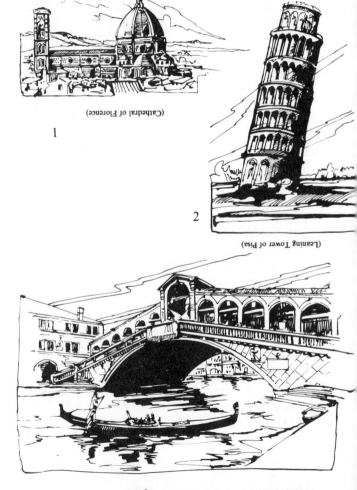

(Cathedral of Florence)

1

2

(Leaning Tower of Pisa)

3 (Rialto Bridge)

4   You are going to the theatre. Your friend asks what
    time the performance starts. What does he say?

5   Tell him it starts at 7 o'clock.

You go to a museum. Which sign do you look for:

6   to find the entrance?

7   to discover the opening times?

8   to buy admission tickets?

9   to find the exit?

10 It is Monday and the museum is shut. What does the
    sign say?

- **Museums** are usually open from 09.00 to 16.00 on
  weekdays and from 09.00 to 13.00 on Saturdays.
  Opening days and hours vary but many are closed on
  Mondays. Many churches are open only in the
  morning.

- **Cinemas** in Italy run continuous performances and
  you can enter at any time. Usually films are dubbed in
  Italian.

- There are some very famous **theatres** in Italy, some of
  which also house the local opera company. In the
  Summer there are open-air performances of operas in,
  for example, the Arena at Verona. Some towns have
  become particularly famous for their International
  Arts Festival, as the Festival dei due Mondi at Spoleto.
  For details and dates it is best to consult the local
  tourist office.

- **Football matches** are played on Sunday afternoons
  (except for international matches).

16 Excursions and Recreation

a. Excursions **b.** Scenery **c.** Sports
d. Photography

a.	l'	**escursione**	*excursion*
	la	**gita**	*trip*
	il	**giro**	*tour*

La gita turistica.	*Tourist excursion.*
La gita in montagna.	*Mountain excursion.*

b.	il	**mare**	*sea*
	il	**golfo**	*gulf*
	l'	*isola*	*island*
	la	**penisola**	*peninsula*
	la	**costa**	*coast*
		pescare	*to fish*
	il	**lago**	*lake*
	il	**fiume**	*river*

il	**monte**	*mountain*
la	**montagna**	*mountains*
il	**passo**	*mountain pass*
il	**vulcano**	*volcano*
la	**grotta**	*cave, grotto*

Mare Adriatico.	*Adriatic Sea.*
L'isola d'Elba.	*Island of Elba.*
Lago di Garda.	*Lake Garda.*
Il Vesuvio è un vulcano.	*Vesuvius is a volcano.*
La Grotta Azzurra.	*Blue Grotto.*

c.

la	**spiaggia**	*beach*
la	**piscina**	*swimming pool*
	nuotare	*to swim*
la	**sedia a sdraio**	*deck chair*
il	**moscone**	*pedal boat*
il	**canotto pneumatico**	*rubber dinghy*
la	**gondola**	*gondola*
la	**barca**	*boat*
il	**windsurf**	*sail board*
il	**motoscafo**	*motorboat*
il	**tennis**	*tennis*
	camminare	*to hike*
l'	**alpinismo**	*mountain climbing*
	sciare	*to ski*
lo	**sci**	*ski, skiing*

Andiamo alla spiaggia.	*We are going to the beach.*
Noleggio barche.	*Boat rental.*
Vorrei noleggiare . . .	*I'd like to hire . . .*
Il campo da tennis.	*Tennis court.*

d.

la	**macchina fotografica**	*camera*
la	**pellicola**	*film*
il	**flash**	*flash*
la	**pila, batteria**	*battery*
la	**foto**	*photo*
la	**diapositiva**	*slide*

E permesso fotografare?	*May I take a picture?*
La pellicola per diapositive.	*Slide film.*

Clothing→19

16   Excursions and Recreation

What do you see in the pictures? Answer in Italian, beginning
with **Vedo** . . . (1 see . . .)

1. . . . .
(il Vesuvio)

2. . . . .
(la Grotta Azzurra)

3. . . . .
(il lago di Garda)

4   What sign do you look for if you want to go to
    (*a*) the beach; (*b*) the swimming pool?
5   Say you would like to hire a surfboard.

You want to buy the following objects. Ask for them
in Italian, beginning **Vorrei** . . . (I would like . . .)

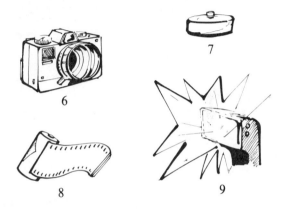

6

7

8

9

- Towns such as Florence and Venice are very popular
  during the Spring and Summer and it is always
  advisable to book a hotel in advance. The same applies
  to most popular resorts in the Alps or on the Coast.
- **Beaches** It is customary for a charge to be made for
  the use of beach facilities such as changing rooms
  (**cabine**), showers, sun umbrellas and deck-chairs.
  There is, however, always a portion of every beach
  which may be used free of charge, but without facilities.
- Public Holidays are as follows:

  1 January (New year's Day)
  Easter Monday
  25 April (Liberation Day)
  1 May (Labour day)
  15 August (Ferragosto)
  1 November (All Saints)
  8 December (Immaculate Conception)
  Christmas Day, Boxing Day

17 The Weather

a. The Weather **b.** Good Weather
c. Bad Weather **d.** Cold Weather

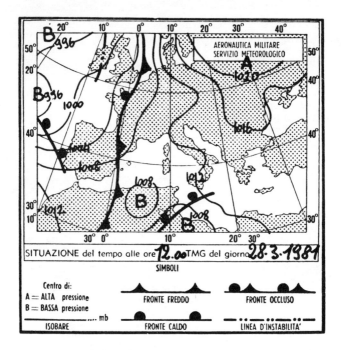

SITUAZIONE del tempo alle ore *12.00* TMG del giorno *28.3.1981*

SIMBOLI

Centro di:
A = ALTA pressione
B = BASSA pressione

FRONTE FREDDO

FRONTE OCCLUSO

_____ .... mb

ISOBARE

FRONTE CALDO

LINEA D'INSTABILITÀ'

AERONAUTICA MILITARE
SERVIZIO METEOROLOGICO

a.	il	**tempo**	*weather*
	le	**previsioni del tempo**	*weather forecast*

Il tempo previsto.	*Today's weather.*
Che tempo farà domani?	*What is the weather for tomorrow?*

b.		**bel tempo**	*good weather*
	il	**sole**	*sun*
		sereno	*clear, bright*
	la	**temperatura**	*temperature*
		caldo	*warm, hot*
		Alta pressione (A)	*high pressure area*

	Il cielo è sereno.	*The sky is clear.*
	C'è sole.	*The sun is shining.*
	Fa caldo.	*It's hot.*
	Ci sono trenta gradi all' ombra.	*It is 30 degrees in the shade.*
	L'acqua è calda.	*The water is warm.*

c.

	Bassa pressione (B)	*low pressure area*
	brutto tempo	*bad weather*
il	**tempo variabile**	*changeable weather*
la	**foschia**	*haze*
la	**nebbia**	*fog*
	nuvoloso	*cloudy*
	poco nuvoloso	*partly cloudy*
la	**nuvola**	*cloud*
la	**nuvolosità**	*amount of cloud*
	coperto	*overcast*
le	**precipitazioni**	*precipitation*
la	**pioggia**	*rain*
i	**rovesci**	*showers*
il	**temporale**	*thunderstorm*
l'	**ombrello**	*umbrella*
il	**vento**	*wind*
la	**schiarita**	*clearing, improvement*

C'è vento.	*It is windy.*
Il vento moderato.	*Moderate wind.*
Il vento molto forte.	*Very strong wind.*
Il mare calmo.	*Calm sea.*
Il mare mosso.	*Rough sea.*
Il mare agitato.	*Stormy sea.*
Piove.	*It is raining.*

d.

	freddo	*cold*
la	**neve**	*snow*
la	**grandine**	*hail*
il	**gelo**	*frost, ice*

Fa freddo.	*It is cold.*
Nevicate.	*Snowfall.*
Le catene de neve.	*Tyre chains.*

17 The Weather

Look at this weather map from an Italian newspaper **Corriere della Sera**:

1 What is the weather like in the Alps?
2 How is the weather in Rome?
3 What is the weather like in the south of Italy?
4 How is the wind in all of Italy?
5 What are the sea conditions in the northern Adriatic?

6 You would like to have some warm water. Which tap do you turn on? (The right **a destra** or the left **a sinistra**?)

What is the weather like?

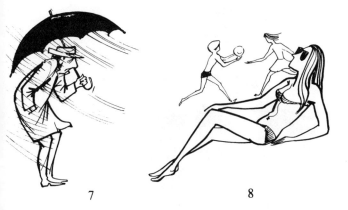

7 8

9 How do you say *It is cold?*

10 How do you ask what the weather will be like tomorrow?

11 What does this traffic sign mean? (Say it in English.)

CON PIOGGIA O GELO

– The vocabulary in this unit is enough to enable you to read the weather forecast in an Italian newspaper.

18 Post Office and Telephone

a. Post Office   **b.** Letters and Postcards
c. Telephone

a.

la	**posta**	*post office*
la	**buca delle lettere**	*letter-box*

Scusi, signora, dov'è la posta?	*Excuse me, where is the post office?*

b.

la	**lettera**	*letter*
la	**busta**	*envelope*
la	**cartolina**	*postcard*
l'	**indirizzo**	*address*
il	**mittente**	*sender*
il	**numero di codice**	*post code*
il	**francobollo**	*stamp*
il	**modulo**	*form*
il	**telegramma**	*telegram*
la	**penna a sfera**	*ballpoint (pen)*

Quanto costa una cartolina per Inghilterra?	*How much is a postcard to England?*
Tre francobolli da quattrocento lire per favore.	*Three 400 lire stamps, please.*
Fare un telegramma.	*To send a telegram.*

c.

il	**telefono**	*telephone, telephone box*
il	**numero**	*telephone number*
il	**centralinista**	*operator*
il	**gettone**	*telephone token*
l'	**elenco telefonico**	*telephone book*
	chiamare	*to telephone*
il	**prefisso**	*area code (number)*

Pronto, a chi parlo?	*Hello, who's calling?*
È il 24–75–23?	*Is that 24–75–23?*
Un attimo.	*One moment.*
Attenda in linea.	*Hold the line, please.*

18 Post Office and Telephone

What are these called in Italian?

7 You want to know the postage to Canada. What do
   you ask for?

8 You want to know the postage to England. What do
   you say?

9 You want three 150 lire stamps. What do you say?

10 You ring the operator who asks you to hold the line. What does she say?

11 You telephone someone. When he answers what does he say?

- Italian **letter boxes** have two slots, one for local mail (**per la città**) and one for other destinations (**per tutte le altre destinazioni**).
- **Telephone tokens (gettoni telefonici)** are needed to make a call. You can get them at the post office, in bars and from machines. Sometimes they are given to you as change when you buy something.
- The person who answers the phone says **pronto,** which is equivalent to hello.
- When you see **Teleselezione** outside a telephone booth, it means that you can dial direct without the operator's assistance.
- In Italy the **yellow pages** are called **Pagine Gialle**.
- One can **telephone to the U.K.** directly by dialling 0044 followed by the exchange code minus the first 0 and then the number. For all enquiries dial 113.

19 Clothing and Toiletries

a. Clothing. **b.** Socks and Shoes **c.** Colours.
d. Toiletries **e.** Hair Care.

a.		**Abbigliamento**	*Clothes*
		Maglieria	*Knitwear*
	la	**giacca di lana**	*cardigan*
	il	**pullover**	*pullover, sweater*
	il	**vestito**	*dress*
	la	**camicetta**	*blouse*
	la	**camicia**	*shirt*
	la	**gonna**	*skirt*
	la	**giacca**	*jacket*
	la	**manica**	*sleeve*
	i	**pantaloni**	*trousers*
	la	**cintura**	*belt*
	il	**cappello**	*hat*
	il	**costume da bagno**	*swimming costume*
	il	**bikini**	*bikini*
	i	**calzoncini da bagno**	*bathing trunks*

Abbigliamento uomo/donna/bambini.	*Men's/Women's/Children's wear.*
Vorrei una camicetta.	*I would like a blouse.*
Che taglia ha?	*What size do you take?*
Posso provarla?	*Can I try it on?*

È troppo larga/stretta.	*It's too big/tight.*
È troppo corta/lunga.	*It's too short/long.*
Va bene.	*This one fits.*
(Non)mi piace.	*I (don't) like it.*
(Non)mi piacciono.	*I (don't) like them.*
La prendo.	*I'll take it.*
Ha qualcosa di più grande/piccolo?	*Have you anything bigger/ smaller?*

b.

le	**scarpe**	*shoes*
le	**calzini**	*socks*
i	**calze**	*stockings*
il	**collant**	*tights*

Che misura?	*What size?*
Ho il numero 38.	*I take a 38.*

c.

il	**colore**	*colour*
	bianco, nero	*white, black*
	grigio, marrone	*grey, brown*
	rosso, verde	*red, green*
	blu, giallo	*blue, yellow*

d.

il	**sapone**	*soap*
l'	**asciugamano**	*towel*
il	**dentifricio**	*toothpaste*
lo	**spazzolino da denti**	*toothbrush*
il	**rasoio elettrico**	*electric razor*
il	**fazzoletto**	*handkerchief*
gli	**assorbenti**	*sanitary towels*
la	**crema solare**	*suntan cream*
il	**latte solare**	*suntan lotion*
gli	**occhiali**	*glasses*
il	**pettine**	*comb*
gli	**occhiali da sole.**	*sunglasses*

e.

il	**barbiere**	*barber*
il	**parrucchiere**	*hairdresser*

Shampoo e messa in piega.	*Shampoo and set, please.*
Mi tagli i capelli, per favore.	*Haircut, please.*

Money, Shopping→ 9

19 Clothing and Toiletries

1 You are in a shop and you try on the following clothes. What are they?

(a)   (b)   (c)

2 What are the following items?

(a)   (b)   (c)

3 Say you like the hat.

4 What are the following items?

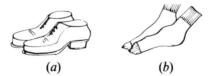

(a)   (b)

5 Say you don't like the shoes.

6 You go into a store and see this sign:

UOMO
primo piano

What does it mean? (Say it in English.)

7 Tell the assistant you would like to buy a white shirt.

8 Say the shirt is too short.

9 Ask the assistant if he has anything bigger.

10 How does the assistant ask what size you take?

11 What are these called in Italian?

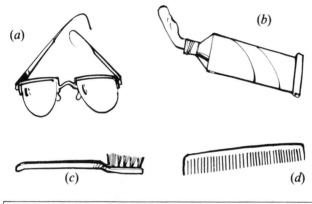

(a)

(b)

(c)

(d)

– When buying **clothes** or **shoes**, remember that Italian sizes are different from British ones.

Shoe sizes

British	1	2		3	4	5	6		7	8	9	10	11	12
Italian	33	34–35		36	37	38	39–40		41	42	43	44	45	46

Dress sizes

British	10	12	14	16	18	20
Italian	38	40	42	44	46	48

Collar sizes

British	13	13½	14	14½	15	15½	16	16½	17
Italian	33	34	35–36	37	38	39	41	42	43

Suits, coats

British	36	38	40	42	44	46
Italian	46	48	50	52	54	56

20 Accidents and Emergencies

a. Breakdowns, Accidents **b.** Theft **c.** Police
d. Doctor **e.** Illness **f.** Chemist **g.** Help

a.

il	**guasto**	*breakdown*
la	**panna di gomma**	*puncture*
l'	**incidente**	*accident*
il	**soccorso stradale**	*emergency service (auto club)*
l'	**officina**	*garage*
il	**danno**	*damage*
l'	**assicurazione**	*insurance*
la	**carta verde**	*insurance papers (green card)*

La macchina non parte.	*The car won't start.*
Chiami il soccorso stradale.	*Call the emergency service.*
La colpa non è mia.	*It's not my fault.*

b.

	articoli de valore	*valuables*
	perdere	*to lose*
	rubare	*to steal*
il	**furto**	*theft*

Ho perso la chiave.	*I've lost my key.*
Bagagli smarriti.	*Lost property.*
Mi è stato rubato il portafoglio.	*Someone stole my wallet.*
Il furto della macchina.	*Car theft.*

c.

la	**polizia (urbana)**	*(urban) police*
i	**carabinieri**	*national police*
la	**questura**	*police headquarters*
la	**denuncia**	*report*
l'	**avvocato**	*lawyer*

Chiami subito la polizia.	*Call the police immediately.*
Fare la denuncia.	*To report to the police.*

	il	**medico**	*doctor*
	il	**dentista**	*dentist*
	l'	**ambulanza**	*ambulance*
	l'	**ospedale**	*hospital*

FARMACIA

Presto, un medico!	*Get a doctor, quick!*
Non c è niente di grave.	*It isn't serious*

		malato	*ill, sick*
	la	**scottatura solare**	*sunburn*
	l'	**indigestione**	*indigestion*
	l'	**attacco cardiaco**	*heart attack*

Sono malato.	*I am sick*
Non posso dormire.	*I can't sleep.*
Ho mal di testa.	*I have a headache*
Ho mal di stomaco.	*I have stomach-ache.*
Ho la febbre.	*I have a fever.*
Mi sono ferito.	*I'm injured.*
Mi sono bruciato la mano.	*I have burnt my hand.*
Mi sono tagliato il dito.	*I have cut my finger.*
Ho mal di denti.	*I have toothache.*

	la	**farmacia**	*chemist, pharmacy*
	la	**ricetta**	*prescription*
	la	**pomata**	*cream, ointment*
	la	**pastiglia**	*pill*
	i	**sonniferi**	*sleeping pills*
	il	**cerotto**	*plaster*
	la	**garza**	*bandage*

Dov' è una farmacia?	*Where is a chemist?*
La farmacia di turno.	*Duty chemist.*
Pronto soccorso.	*First aid; Casualty Dept*

	il	**pericolo**	*danger*
		attenzione	*watch out*

Aiuto!	*Help!*
La cintura di sicurezza.	*Safety belt.*

1   You are telephoning a garage. Tell the mechanic your car won't start.

2   You are involved in an accident. How do you ask someone to call the Police?

3   You were not to blame for the accident. What do you tell the Police?

4   You witnessed an accident. How do you ask someone to call the emergency services?

5   Tell the Police you have lost your wallet.

6   Say someone has stolen your suitcase.

7   You are not feeling well and you go to a doctor. Tell the doctor you have (*a*) a headache; (*b*) stomach ache; (*c*) burnt your finger; (*d*) cut your hand.

8   The doctor does not think it is serious. What does he say?

9   Ask the chemist for
(*a*) some   ointment;   (*b*) some   sticking-plasters;
(*c*) some sleeping-pills.

10   Tell the dentist you have toothache.

Accidents and Emergencies 20

- There are emergency telephones on motorways and calls are handled by the ACI (Italian Automobile Club). The breakdown service is free to foreign visitors who have obtained a **carta carburante.** On ordinary roads, dial 116 at the nearest telephone and give the operator the relevant details. The ACI will be immediately informed.

- Visitors to Italy from Britain have the right to the same **health facilities** as Italians. Form E111 should be obtained from the Department of Health and Social Security before leaving for Italy. Treatment is free apart from services for which Italians, too, must pay (prescription fees, private dental treatment, etc.) Keep receipts for refunds.

- At every **chemist (farmacia**–recognised by the Red Cross symbol displayed outside) there is a list of those open at night and on Sundays. Chemists also stock baby foods and sanitary goods.

- In resorts **emergency treatment** is offered by the **Guardia Medica**, where a doctor is always on call. For emergencies and hospital treatment ask for **Pronto Soccorso** (Casualty) at the nearest hospital.

- Here is a list of useful words:
  Farmacia *Chemist*
  Dottore/Medico *Doctor*
  Infermiere/Infermiera *Nurse*
  il dito *finger*
  le gambe *legs*
  i piedi *feet*
  i denti *teeth*

  and some common ailments:
  la scottatura *sunburn*
  l'insolazione *sunstroke*
  l'indigestione *indigestion*
  l'intossicazione *food-poisoning*
  la puntura d'insetto *insect bite*
  la febbre *fever*
  la tosse *cough*

Answers

1 General Expressions
1 Buongiorno, signore. 2 Buona sera, signora. 3 Molto bene, grazie, e lei? *or* Non c'è male. 4 Arrivederla, signore. 5 Ciao, Luigi. 6 Sono la signora Marshall. 7 Il passaporto, per favore. 8 Questa valigia? 9 Sì, è la mia valigia. 10 No, non è la mia valigia. 11 Scusi, signora. 12 Grazie, signore. 13 Mia moglie.

2 Arriving in Italy
1 La valigia (una valigia) 2 La borsetta (una borsetta). 3 No, nulla da dichiarare. 4 Apra il portabagagli, per favore. 5 Apra la valigia, per favore. 6 Sì, sono inglese. 7 Mi chiamo . . .
8 La sua patente, per favore. 9 Buon viaggio.
10 Non capisco. 11 Parla inglese? 12 La Gran Bretagna.
13 L' Australia. 14 L' Italia. 15 Ha riviste inglesi?

3 Driving a Car
1 La macchina (una macchina). 2 La roulotte (una roulotte). 3 Autonoleggio. 4 Quanto? 5 Venti litri di super, per favore. 6 Mi faccia il pieno, per favore. 7 Controlli l'olio e le gomme, per favore. 8 Alla stazione di servizio.
9 L'autostrada. 10 Il parcheggio. 11 La stazione di servizio *or* la benzina.

4 Finding your way
1 Nord, sud, est, ovest. 2 Una pianta di Pisa, per favore.
3 Una carta stradale, per favore. 4 Avanti. 5 Alt.
6 Dov' è la via Manzini? 7 Giri a destra. 8 A destra.
9 Giri a sinistra. 10 Vada sempre diritto. 11 È lontano?
12 È la prima strada a destra. 13 Centro città.

5 Public Transport
1 Informazioni. 2 Partenze internazionali. 3 Consegna bagagli. 4 Arrivi. 5 Un traghetto. 6 Un aliscafo.
7 Padova. 8 Venezia S. Lucia. 9 Return ticket (andata e ritorno) 10 Un biglietto per Venezia, andata e ritorno, per favore. 11 Da che binario parte? 12 È un rapido o un expresso? 13 All' hotel Victoria, per favore. 14 Fermi qui, per favore.

6 Accommodation
1 Il letto (un letto) 2 La chiave (una chiave) 3 C'è un hotel qui vicino? 4 Ha una camera libera? 5 Ho prenotato una camera per una settimana. 6 Una camera doppia per due notti, per favore. 7 Una camera singola con bagno, per favore. 8 Una

camera a due letti con doccia, per favore. 9 Quanto costa la camera? 10 È troppo cara. 11 T (Pianterreno) 12 La doccia non funziona. 13 Mi faccia il conto, per favore. 14 Un campeggio. 15 Dov'è l' ostello della gioventù, per favore?

7 Numbers, Weights and Measures

1 Numero quindici. 2 Numero ventisette. 3 Numero centodieci. 4 Numero duecentododici. 5 Cinque. 6 Tre. 7 Sei. 8 Sei. 9 Due. 10 (a) trecento chilometri; (b) trecentocinquanta chilometri; (c) quattrocentosessanta chilometri; (d) settecentoquaranta chilometri; (e) novecentocinquanta chilometri; (f) millecinquanta chilometri. 11 Quattromilacento lire. 12 Mezzo chilo di pomodori, per favore. 13 Due etti e mezzo di burro, per favore. 14 Un chilo di pasta, per favore.

8 Times and Dates

1 (a) un' ora; (b) mezz'ora; (c) quarto d'ora. 2 (a) la mattina; (b) il pomeriggio; (c) la notte. 3 (a) un giorno; (b) una settimana; (c) un anno. 4 Che ore sono? 5 (a) è l'una; (b) sono le due; (c) sono le sei; (d) sono le sei e mezzo; (e) sono le sei e un quarto; (f) sono le sei meno un quarto. 6 No. 7 No. 8 Parto a mezzanotte. 9 A che ora parte l'aereo? 10 Arriva alle sette di sera.

9 Money and Shopping

1 La Banca. 2 Vorrei cambiare cento sterline in lire. 3 Che cosa desidera? 4 Vorrei una borsetta. 5 Ha una borsetta bianca? 6 Quanto costa? 7 Mi piace questa borsetta. 8 6.440 = Seimilaquattrocentoquaranta lire. 9 10.000 = Diecimila. 10 3.560 = Tremilacinquecentosessanta. 11 cinquecentosettanta; novecento; cinquecentosettanta; centocinquanta; milleottocento; millecinquecentocinquanta; settecentoventi; centocinquanta; trenta. 12 Qual cosa d'altro? 13 Grazie, basta così. 14 L'offerta speciale.

10 Meals

1 La colazione, il pranzo, la cena. 2 (a) la forchetta; (b) il piatto; (c) il coltello; (d) il cucchiaio; (e) il bicchiere; (f) la bottiglia. 3 Caffè e latte. 4 (a) il pane; (b) il salame; (c) il prosciutto. 5 Un bicchiere di vino, per favore. 6 Una tazza di tè, per favore. 7 Un caffelatte, per favore. 8 Una pizza ai funghi, per favore,

11 Restaurants

1 (a) un ristorante o una trattoria; (b) un bar o un caffè; (c) un caffè; (d) una pizzeria. 2 È libero questo posto? 3 Un tavolo per tre persone, per favore, 4 Cameriere, il menù, per favore. 5 Prendo il piatto del giorno. 6 E da bere? 7 (a) il

sale e il pepe; (b) l'olio e l'aceto. 8 Cameriere, mi porta l'olio e l'aceto, per favore. 9 Il conto, per favore. 10 Questo è per lei.

12 Pasta, Meat, Fish
1 La carne. 2 Il pollo. 3 Il pesce. 4 La pasta. 5 Zuppa di verdura, per favore. 6 Spaghetti alla bolognese, per favore. 7 Zuppa di pesce, per favore. 8 Cotoletta alla milanese, per favore. 9 Fegato fritto, per favore 10 Pollo arrosto, per favore. 11 Filetti di merluzzo, per favore. 12 Uova al prosciutto, per favore.

13 Vegetables, Fruit, Desserts
1 I fagioli. Mi piacciono i fagioli. 2 La cipolla. Mi piace la cipolla. 3 Le carote. Mi piacciono le carote. 4 Le patate. Mi piacciono le patate. 5 Gli asparagi. Mi piacciono gli asparagi. 6 Il carciofo. Mi piace il carciofo. 7 Il pomodoro. Mi piace il pomodoro. 8 La mela. Mi piace la mela. 9 Il melone. Mi piace il melone. 10 Un' insalata verde, per favore. 11 Melone e prosciutto, per favore. 12 Macedonia con panna, per favore. 13 (a) un gelato con panna, per favore; (b) un gelato alla vaniglia, per favore; (c) un gelato di limone per favore; (d) un gelato di fragole, per favore.

14 Drinking and Smoking
1 Un cappuccino, per favore. 2 Un espresso, per favore. 3 Acqua minerale non gassata, per favore. 4 Succo di pomodoro, per favore. 5 Un quarto di vino bianco, per favore. 6 Una birra, per favore. 7 Vorrei una bottiglia di vino da tavola. 8 Vorrei una bottiglia di vino bianco. 9 Vorrei una grappa. 10 (a) un pacchetto di sigarette; (b) una scatola di fiammiferi; (c) un accendino; (d) un' apribottiglia; (e) una bottiglia.

15 Sightseeing and Entertainment
1 Il duomo di Firenze. 2 La torre di Pisa. 3 Il ponte di Rialto. 4 A che ora comincia lo spettacolo? 5 Comincia alla sette. 6 L'entrata. 7 L'orario. 8 La cassa. 9 L'uscita. 10 Chiuso.

16 Excursions and Recreation
1 Vedo il Vesuvio. 2 Vedo la Grotta Azzurra. 3 Vedo il Lago di Garda. 4 (a) la spiaggia; (b) la piscina. 5 Vorrei noleggiare un windsurf. 6 Vorrei una macchina fotografica. 7 Vorrei una pila. 8 Vorrei una pellicola. 9 Vorrei un flash.

17 The Weather
1 C'è nebbia. 2 C'è sereno. 3 C'è pioggia. 4 Il vento è moderato. 5 Poco mosso. 6 A sinistra (caldo). 7 Piove e c'è

vento. 8 C'è sole e fa caldo. 9 Fa freddo. 10 Che tempo farà domani? 11 Slippery if wet or icy.

18 Post Office and Telephone

1 Una cartolina. 2 Una buca delle lettere. 3 Una busta. 4 L'indirizzo. 5 Il francobollo. 6 Una penna (a sfera) 7 Quanto costa un francobollo per il Canadà? 8 Quanto costa un francobollo per l'Inghilterra? 9 Tre francobolli da centocinquanta lire, per favore. 10 Attenda in linea, per favore. 11 Pronto, a chi parla?

19 Clothing and Toiletries

1 (*a*) una camicetta; (*b*) una camicia; (*c*) una giacca. 2 (*a*) una cintura; (*b*) i calzoncini da bagno; (*c*) un cappello. 3 Mi piace il cappello. 4 (*a*) le scarpe; (*b*) i calzini. 5 Non mi piacciono le scarpe. 6 Menswear. First floor. 7 Vorrei una camicia bianca. 8 Questa camicia è troppo corta. 9 Ha qualcosa di più grande? 10 Che taglia ha? 11 (*a*) gli occhiali. (*b*) il dentifricio; (*c*) uno spazzolino da denti; (*d*) il pettine;

20 Accidents and Emergencies

1 La macchina non parte. 2 Chiami la polizia, per favore. 3 La colpa non è mia. 4 Chiami il soccorso stradale. 5 Ho il portafoglio. 6 Mi è stata rubata la valigia. 7 (*a*) ho mal di testa (*b*) ho mal di stomaco; (*c*) mi sono bruciato il dito; (*d*) mi sono tagliato la mano. 8 Non c'è niente di grave. 9 (*a*) una pomata, per favore; (*b*) una scatola di cerotti, per favore; (*c*) dei sonniferi, per favore. 10 Ho mal di denti.

Italian – English Vocabulary

abbiglimento clothes, wear 19a
accendere to turn on 3b
accendino lighter 14c
aceto vinegar 11c
acqua water 17b
acqua minerale mineral water 14a
a destra to the right 4d
aereo aeroplane 5b
aeroporto airport 5b
affresco fresco 15b
agenzia di viaggi travel agency 15a
agnello lamb 12b
aiuto help 20g
albergo inn, hotel 6a
alimentari groceries 9
aliscafo hydrofoil 5c
alpinismo mountain climbing 16c
alt stop, wait 4c
alta pressione high pressure 17b
amaro bitters 14b
ambasciata embassy 2c
ambulanza ambulance 20d
americano American 2c
andare drive (to) 3a, go (to) 3a
andata e ritorno return ticket 5e
anno year 8c
antipasto starter 11b
aperto open 15d
aprire to open 15d
apribottiglia bottle opener 14b
arancia orange 13b
arco arch 15b
area di servizio service area 3b
arrivi arrivals 5e
arrivederci, arrivederla goodbye 1b
arrosto roasted 12c
articoli di valore valuables 20b
ascensore lift 6b
asciugamano towel 19d
a sinistra to the left 4d
asparagi asparagus 13a
assicurazione insurance 20a
assorbenti sanitary towels 19d
attacco cardiaco heart attack 20e
attenzione watch out, be careful 3b/20g
Australia Australia 2c
Australiano Australian 2c

autocarro lorry 3a
autonoleggio car rental 3a
autostrada motorway 3b
avanti go 4c
avvocato lawyer 20c
azienda di soggiorno Tourist Information Bureau 15a

baccalà dried cod 12d
bagaglio luggage 1f/2a
bagno bath 6b
bambino child 1d/19a
bar bar, café 11a
barbiere barber 19e
barca boat 16c
bassa pressione low pressure 17c
bello beautiful 17b
bene good 19a
benzina petrol 3c
bere to drink 10a, 11b
bevande beverages, drinks 14a
bianco white 9c/19c
bicchiere glass 10b
biglietteria ticket counter 5e
biglietto ticket, banknote 5e, 9a
biglietto d'ingresso admission ticket 15d
binario platform 5a
birra beer 14b
biscotti biscuits 13c
bistecca steak 12b
blu blue 19c
borsetta handbag 2a
bottiglia bottle 10b/14b
braciola chop 12b
brutto bad 17c
buca delle lettere letter-box 18a
buona sera good evening 1b
buon giorno good morning, hello 1b
buono good 2a/6a/11b
burro butter 7b, 10c

caduta massi rockfall 3b
caffè cafeteria 11a
    coffee 10b/14a
caffelatte coffee w. milk 10c

Italian – English Vocabulary

calamari squid 12d
caldo warm, hot 17b
calmo calm 17c
calze stockings 19b
calzini socks 19b
calzoncini da bagno bathing trunks 19a
cambio change, rate of exchange 9b
camera room 6b/10a
cameriere waiter 11d
camicetta blouse 19a
camicia shirt 9c/19a
campanile bell tower 15b
campeggio campsite 6a
campo da tennis tennis court 16c
Canada Canada 2c
canadese Canadian 2c
canotto pneumatico rubber dinghy 16c
cappello hat 19a
carabinieri police 20c
caraffa jug 10b
carciofo artichoke 13a
carne meat 12b
caro expensive 6c/9d
carote carrots 13a
carrozza cuccette couchette 5a
carrozza letti sleeping car 5a
carrozza ristorante dining car 5a
carta map 4a
carta di credito credit card 9b
carta verde car insurance paper 20a
cartolina postcard 18b
casa house 4b
cassa cashier 9d, ticket window 15d
castello castle 15b
catena da neve snow chain 17d
cavatappl corkscrew 14b
cavolfiore cauliflower 13a
c'è there is 1e/6a/17c/20f
cena dinner 10a
cenare to have dinner 10a
centralinista telephone operator 18c
centro città town centre 4b
cerotto plaster 20f
chiamare to call 2b; telephone 18c
chiamarsi to be called 2b

chiave key 1e/1f/6b/20b
chiesa church 15b
chilo kilo 7b
chilometro kilometre 7b
chiudere to close 15d
chiuso closed 8c/15d
ci sono there are 1e
cielo sky 17b
cintura belt 19a
cintura di sicurezza safety belt 20g
cioccolata chocolate, cocoa (drink) 13c
cioccolato chocolate 13c
cipolla onion 13a
città city 4b
cognome surname 2b
colazione breakfast 10a
collant tights 19b
colore colour 19c
coltello knife 10b
comprare to buy 9c
comune municipality, town hall 4b
con with 6b/13a/13b/13c/18c
consegna bagagli baggage collection 5b
consolato consulate 2c
conto bill 6c, 11d
contorni vegetables 13a
controllare to check 3c
controllo passaporti passport control 2b
controllo sicurezza security control 5b
coperto cover charge 11b; overcast 17c
coppa bowl of ice cream 13c
corriera coach 5d
corso avenue 4c
corto short 19a
costare to cost 9d
costa coast 16b
cotoletta escalope 12b
costume da bagno bathing costume 19a
cozze mussels 12d
crema solare suntan cream 19d
cucchiaio spoon 10b
curva bend 4d
custodito guarded 3d

Italian – English Vocabulary

danno damage 20a
decaffeinato decaffeinated coffee 14a
denaro money 9a
dentifricio toothpaste 19d
dentista dentist 20d
denuncia report 20c
destinazione destination 5e
deviazione diversion 3b
dichiarare to declare 2a
direzione direction 4d
diritto straight ahead 4d
disco orario parking disc 3d
doccia shower 6b
dogana customs 2a
dolce dessert 11b
domani tomorrow 8b/17a
domenica Sunday 8c
domicilio place of residence 2b
donna woman, lady 1d/19a
dopodomani (the) day after tomorrow 8b
doppio double 6b
dormire to sleep 20e
duomo cathedral 15b

e and 17a
ecco here is 1e/6c
edificio storico historical building 15b
elenco telefonico telephone book 18c
entrata entrance 15d
escursione excursion 16a
est east 4d
etto 100 grams 7b

fagioli beans 13a
fagiolini French beans 13a
fari headlights 3b
farmacia chemist 20f
fazzoletto handkerchief 19d
febbre fever 20e
fegato liver 12b
ferito hurt 20e
fermata (bus) stop 5d
ferrovia railway 5a
fiammiferi matches 14c
filetto fillet 12d
filtro filter 14c

finocchio fennel 13a
firma signature 2b
fiume river 16b
flash flash (bulb) 16d
fontana fountain 15b
forchetta fork 10b
formaggio cheese 11b
forte strong 17c
foschia haze 17c
fotografare to photograph 16d
fragole strawberries 13b
francobollo stamp 18b
freddo cold 17d
fritto fried 12b/12d
frutta fruit 11b/13c
frutti di mare shellfish 12d
frutto fruit 13c
funghi mushrooms 10d
furto robbery 20b

gabinetto toilet 6d
galleria tunnel 3b, art gallery 15b
Galles Wales 2c
gallese Welsh 2c
gamberi prawns 12d
garza bandage 20f
gasolio diesel 3c
gassata carbonated 14a
gelateria ice cream parlour 13c
gelato ice cream 11b/13c
gelo frost, ice 17d
gentile nice 1c
gettone telephone token 18c
giacca jacket 19a
giallo yellow 19c
giornale newspaper 2c
giorno day 1e, 8b
giovedì Thursday 8c
giri turn 4d
giro tour 16a
giro della città city tour 4b/15a
gita trip, excursion 16a
golfo gulf 16b
gomma tyre 3c
gondola gondola 16c
gonna skirt 19a
grado degree 17b
grammo gram 7b

Italian – English Vocabulary

Gran Bretagna Great Britain 2c
grande big 19a
grandi magazzini department store 9c
grandine hail 17d
grappa brandy 14b
grattugliato grated 12a
gratuito free 9d
grave serious 20f
grazie thank you 1c/9c
grigio grey 19c
grotta grotto 16b
guida guide-book 15a

ieri yesterday 8b
il, la the 1e
imbarco embarkment area 5c
incidente accident 20a
indigestione indigestion 20e
indirizzo address 18b
informazione information 5e
inghilterra England 2c
inglese English 2c
ingresso entrance 15d
innocente innocent 20a
insalata salad 13a
isola island 16b
Italia Italy 2c
italiano Italian 2c

lago lake 16b
lana wool 19a
largo big 19a
latte milk 10b/14a
lei you 11d
lento slow 3a
lesso cooked 13b
lettera letter 18b
letto bed 6b
letto matrimoniale double bed 6b
libero free, vacant 6d/11a
libretto di circolazione car registration papers 2b
limonata lemonade 14a
limone lemon 10c/13c
liquore liqueur 14b
litro litre 3c/7b

lontano far 4d
luglio July 8b
lunedì Monday 8c
lungo long 19a

macchina car 3a/20b
macchina fotografica camera 16d
macedonia fruit salad 13b
macelleria butcher's shop 10e
maglieria knitwear 19a
maiale pork 12b
malato ill, sick 20e
mal di denti toothache 20e
mal di stomaco stomach-ache 20e
mal di testa headache 20e
mancia tip 11d
manica sleeve 19a
mangiare to eat 10a
mano hand 20e
manzo beef 12b
mare sea 16b/17c
marito husband 1f
marmellata jam, marmalade 10c
marrone brown 19c
martedì Tuesday 8c
mattina, mattino morning 8b
medico doctor 20d
mela apple 13b
melanzana aubergine 13a
menù menu 11b
mercato market 9c
mercoledì Wednesday 8c
merluzzo cod 12d
mese month 8c
metro metre 7b
mezzo half 7b
mezza pensione half board 10a
mezzanotte midnight 8b
mezzogiorno noon 8b
mezz'ora half an hour 8a
minestra soup 12a
minestrone vegetable soup 13a
mio my 1f
misura size 19b
mittente sender 18b
moderato moderate 17c
moglie wife 1f
molto very much 1c/7b/17c
montagna mountains 16a/16b

Italian – English Vocabulary

monte mountain 16b
mortadella type of sausage 10d
moscone pedal boat 16c
mosso rough 17c
motoscafo motorboat 16c
museo museum 15b

nave ship 5c
nazionalità nationality 2c
nebbia fog 17c
negozio shop 9c
nero black 19c
neve snow 17d
niente nothing 20f
no no 1a/2a
noleggio rental 16c
nome name, first name 1f/2b
non not 1b/2c/9d/20a/20f
normale 2-star 3c
notte night 6b/8b
nulla nothing 2a
numero number 6b/18c
numero di codice post code 18b
nuotare to swim 16c
nuvola cloud 17c
nuvolosità amount of cloud 17c
nuvoloso cloudy 17c

occhiali glasses 19d
occhiali da sole sunglasses 19d
occupato occupied 6d
offerta speciale special offer 9c
officina garage 20a
oggetti goods 2a
oggi today 8b/17a
olio oil 3c/11c
oliva olive 13a
ombra shade 17b
ombrello umbrella 17c
opera opera 15c
opera d'arte work of art 15b
opuscolo brochure 15a
ora hour 8a
orario timetable 5e,
   opening hours 9c/15d
orologio watch, clock 8a
ospedale hospital 20d
ostello della gloventù youth hostel 6a
ovest west 4d

pacchetto packet 14c
palazzo palace 15b
pane bread 10c
panetteria bakery 10e
panino roll 10c
panna fresh cream 13b/13c
pantaloni trousers 19a
parcheggio car-park 3d
parmigiano Parmesan cheese 12a
parrucchiere hairdresser 19e
partenze departures 5b/5e
partita di calcio football match 15b
passaporto passport 1c/2b
passo mountain pass 16b
pasta pasta 7b/12a
pastasciutta noodles 12a
pasticceria pastry shop 11a
pasticcini pastries 13c
pastiglia pill 20f
pasto meal 10a
patate potatoes 13a
patate fritte chips 13a
patente driving licence 2b
pedaggio toll charge 3b
pellicola film 16d
penisola peninsula 16b
penna a sfera ball point pen 18b
pensione completa full board 10a
pepe pepper 11c
peperone pepper 13a
per to, for 3b/5e/11a/11d
perdere to lose 20b
per favore please 1c
pericolo danger 20g
permesso allowed 16d
pesca peach 10c/13b
pescare to fish 16b
pesce fish 12d
pescheria fishmonger 10e
pettine comb 19d
piacere: mi piace I like 9
piano floor 6b
pianta della città city plan 4a
pianterreno ground floor 6b
piatto plate 10b, course 11b
piatto del giorno today's menu 11b
piazza square 4c
piazzale square 4c
piccolo little, small 14b

Italian – English Vocabulary

pieno full 3c
pila battery 16d
pioggia rain 17c
piscina swimming pool 16c
piselli peas 13a
poco little 7b
polizia police 20c
pollo chicken 12c
pollo novello young chicken 12c
pomata ointment, cream 20f
pomeriggio afternoon 8b
pomodoro tomato 12b/13a
ponte bridge 4c/15b, deck 5c
portabagagli car boot 2a
portacenere ashtray 14c
portafoglio wallet 20b
portare to bring 11c
porto port 5c
posta post office 18a
posto seat 11a
pranzare to have lunch 10a
pranzo lunch 10a
precipitazione precipitation 17c
prefisso area code 18c
prego don't mention it 1c
prenotare to book 6b
prenotazione reservation 5e
presto quick 20f
previsioni del tempo weather forecast 17a
prezzo price 6c/9d
pronto hello 18c
pronto soccorso first aid 20e
prosciutto ham 10d/12b/12c/13a
prossimo next 8c
provenlenza origin 5e
pullman coach 5d
pullover sweater 19a

quadro painting 15b
qualcosa something 2a
quando when 8a/8b
quanto how much 3c/7b/9d/18b
quarto one quarter 8a/14b
questo this 1e/11d
questura police headquarters 20b
qui here 5d/6a

ragazzo boy; **ragazza** girl 1d
rallentare slow down 3a
rasoio elettrico electric shaver 19d
ricetta prescription 20f
ricevimento reception 6
ricevuta receipt 11d
riduzione discount 5e
riso rice 13a
ristorante restaurant 11a
ritardo delay 5e
rivista magazine 2c
rosso red 19c
roulotte caravan 3c
rovesci showers 17c
rubare to steal 20b

sabato Saturday 8c
sala da pranzo dining room 10a
salame salami 10d
sale salt 11c
salsa sauce 12b
sapone soap 19d
scala stairs 6b
scaloppina cutlet 12b
scarpe shoes 19b
scatola box 14c
schiarita clearing 17c
sci ski, skiing 16c
sciare to ski 16c
scorso last 8c
scottatura solare sunburn 20e
Scozia Scotland 2c
scozzese Scottish 2c
sedia a sdraio deck chair 16b
semaforo traffic light 4c
sempre always 4c
senso unico one-way street 3b
senza without 14c
sera evening 8a/8b
sereno clear, bright 17b
settimana week 8c
sì yes 1a/2c
sigaretta cigarette 14c
sigaro cigar 14c
signora Mrs. 1d/6d
signore Mr. 1d/6d
signorina Miss 1d
singolo single 6b

Italian – English Vocabulary

soccorso stradale emergency service 20a
sogliola sole 12d
soldi money 9a
sole sun 17b
sonniferi sleeping pills 20e
spazzolino da denti toothbrush 19d
spettacolo performance 15c
spiaggia beach 16c
spiccioli small change 9a
spinaci spinach 13a
spingere to push, to press 15d
spremuta fresh fruit juice 14a
spumante sparkling wine 14b
stagione season 8c
stazione station 5a/5d
stazione centrale main station 5a/7b
stazione di servizio service station 3c
sterlina pound sterling 9b
stomaco stomach 20d
strada street 4c, road 3b
stretto narrow, tight 9a
subito quick 20c
succo juice 14a
sud south 4d
sugo tomato sauce 12b
suo your 1f
super 4-star
supermercato supermarket 9c
supplemento surcharge 5e

tabaccheria cigar store 14c
taglia size 19a
tassa d'imbarco airport tax 5b
tassi taxi 5d
tavola, tavolo table 11a
tavola calda snack bar 11a
tazza cup 10b
tè tea 10c/14a
teatro theatre 15c
tempio temple 15b
tempo weather 17a/17b/17c
temporale thunderstorm 17c
terrazza terrace 11a
testa head 20d
tirare to pull 15d
tonno tuna 12d
torre tower 15b

torta cake 13c
tovagliolo napkin 10b
traghetto 1y 5c
tramezzini open sandwiches 10d
trattoria restaurant 11a
treno train 5a
turista tourist 15a
tutto all, everything 6b

ufficio office 15a
un, una a, an 1e
uomo man 1d
uovo egg 12a/12c
uscita exit 3b/15d
uva grape 13b

va bene O.K. 2a
vada go 4d
valigia suitcase 1e/2a
vaniglia vanilla 13c
variabile changeable 17c
vedere to see 16
veicolo vehicle 3a
veloce fast 3a
velocità speed 3a
venerdì Friday 8c
vento wind 17c
verde green 13a/19c
verdura vegetable 12a/13a
vermut vermouth 14b
vestito dress 19a
via street 4c
viaggio trip 2a
viale avenue 4c
vicino near 4d
vietato prohibited 14c/15d
vino wine 10b/14b
visitare to visit 15d
visita con guida guided tour 15d
vitello veal 12b
volo flight 5b
vulcano volcano 16b

windsurf sailboard 16c

zucchero sugar 11c
zuppa soup 12a

English – Italian Vocabulary

a, an un, una 1e
accident incidente 20a
address indirizzo 18b
admission ticket biglietto d'ingresso 15d
aeroplane aereo 5b
afternoon pomeriggio 8b
airport aeroporto 5b
airport tax tassa d'imbarco 5b
all tutto 6b
allowed permesso 16d
always sempre 4c
ambulance ambulanza 20d
American americano 2c
and e 17a
apple mela 13b
arch arco 15b
area code prefisso 18c
arrivals arrivi 5e
art gallery galleria 15b
artichoke carciofo 13a
ashtray portacenere 14c
asparagus asparagi 13a
attention attenzione 3b/20g
aubergine melanzana 13a
avenue viale 4c

bad brutto 17c
baggage collection consegna bagagli 5b
bakery panetteria 10e
bandage garza 20f
bar caffè, bar 11a
barber barbiere 19e
bath bagno 6b
bathing costume costume da bagno 19a
bathing trunks calzoncini da bagno 19a
battery pila 16d
beach spiaggia 16c
beans fagioli 13a
beautiful bello 17b
bed letto 6b
beef manzo 12b
beer birra 14b
bell tower campanile 15b

belt cintura 19a
bend curva 4d
beverages bevande 14a
big largo, grande 19a
bill conto 6c/11d
biscuits biscotti 13c
bitters amaro 14b
black nero 19c
blouse camicetta 19a
blue blu 19c
boat barca 16c
boot (of car) portabagagli 2a
bottle bottiglia 10b/14b
bottle opener apribottiglia 14b
bowl of ice cream coppa 13c
box scatola 14c
boy ragazzo 1d
brandy grappa 14b
bread pane 10c
breakfast colazione; **to have breakfast** far colazione 10a
bridge ponte 4c/15b
bright sereno 17b
brochure opuscolo 15a
brown marrone 19c
butcher's shop macelleria 10e
butter burro 10c
buy (to) comprare 9c

cafeteria caffè 11a
cake torta 13c
call (to) chiamare 2b
calm calmo 17c
camera macchina fotografica 16d
campsite campeggio 6a
Canada Canada 2c
Canadian canadese 2c
car macchina 3a/20b
caravan roulotte 3c
car-park parcheggio 3d
car registration papers libretto di circolazione 2b
car rental autonoleggio 3a
carrots carote 13a
cashier cassa 9d
castle castello 15b

English – Italian Vocabulary

cathedral duomo 15b
cauliflower cavolfiore 13a
caution! attenzione 3b/20g
centro centre 4b
change cambio 9b
changeable variabile 17c
check (to) controllare 3c
chemist farmacia 20f
cheese formaggio 11b
chicken pollo 12c
child bambino 1d/19a
chips patate fritte 13a
chocolate cloccolata, cioccolato 13c
chop braciola 12b
church chiesa 15b
cigar sigaro 14c
cigarette sigaretta 14c
city città 5b
clear sereno 17b
clearing schiarita 17c
closed chiuso 8c/15d
clothes abbigliamento 19a
cloud nuvola 17c
clouding nuvolosità 17c
cloudy nuvoloso 17c
coach pullman, corriera 5d
coast costa 16b
cocoa cioccolata 13c
cod baccalà 12d, merluzzo 12d
coffee caffè 10b/14a
coffee with milk caffelatte 10c
cold freddo 17d
colour colore 19c
comb pettine 19d
consulate consolato 2c
corkscrew cavatappi 14b
couchette carrozza cuccette 5a
course (meal) piatto 11b
cover charge coperto 11b
cream (ointment) pomata 20f
cream (fresh) panna 13c
cup tazza 10b
customs dogana 2a
cutlet scaloppina 12b

damage danno 20a

danger pericolo 20g
day giorno 8b
day after tomorrow dopodomani 8b
decaffeinated coffee decaffeinato 14a
deck ponte 5c
deck chair sedia a sdraio 16b
declare (to) dichiarare 2a
degree grado 17b
delay ritardo 5e
dentist dentista 20d
department store grandi magazzini 9c
departures partenze 5b/5e
dessert dolce 11b
destination destinazione 5e
diesel gasolio 3c
dining car carrozza ristorante 5a
dining room sala da pranzo 10a
dinner cena 10a; **to have dinner** cenare 10a
direction direzione 4d
direct train treno diretto 5a
discount riduzione 5e
diversion deviazione 3b
doctor medico 20d
double bed letto matrimoniale 6b
double room camera doppia 6b
dress vestito 19a
drinks bevande 14a
drive (to) andare 3c
driving licence patente 2b

east est 4d
eat (to) mangiare 10a
egg uovo 12a/12c
electric shaver rasoio elettrico 19d
embarkation area imbarco 5c
embassy ambasciata 2c
emergency service soccorso stradale 20a
England Inghilterra 2c
English inglese 2c
entrance entrata 15d
escalope cotoletta 12b
evening sera 8a/8b
everything tutto 6b
exit uscita 3b/15d
excursion escursione 16a

English – Italian Vocabulary

expensive caro 6c/9d
express train treno rapido 5a

far lontano 4d
fast veloce 3a
fast train treno espresso 5a
fennel finocchio 13a
ferry traghetto 5c
fever febbre 20e
fillet filetti 12d
film pellicola 16d
filtre filtro 14c
first aid pronto soccorso 20e
first name nome 1f/2b
fish pesce 12d
fish (to) pescare 16b
fish market pescheria 10e
flash (bulb) flash 16d
flight volo 5b
floor piano 6b
fog nebbia 17b
football match partita di calcio 15b
for per 3b/5e/11a/11d
fork forchetta 10b
fountain fontana 15b
free gratuito 9d, libero 6d/11a
French beans fagiolini 13a
fresco affresco 15b
Friday venerdì 8c
fried fritto 12b/12d
frost gelo 17d
fruit frutta, frutti 11b/13b/13c
fruit salad macedonia 13b
full pieno 3c
full board pensione completa 10a

garage officina 20a
girl ragazza 1d
glass bicchiere 10b
glasses occhiali 19d
go avanti 4c, andare 3a
gondola gondola 16c
good bene 19a
  buono 2a/6a/11b
goodbye arrivederci, arrivederla, ciao
  1b

good evening buona sera 1b
good morning buon giorno 1b
goods oggetti 2a
gram grammo 7b
grape uva 13b
grated grattugiato 12a
Great Britain Gran Bretagna 2c
green verde 13a/19c
green card carta verde 20a
grey grigio 19c
groceries alimentari 10e
grotto grotta 16b
ground floor pianterreno 6b
guarded custodito 3d
guidebook guida 15a
guest-house pensione 6
guided tour visita con guida 15d
gulf golfo 16b

hail grandine 17d
hairdresser parrucchiere 19e
half mezzo 7b
half an hour mezz'ora 8a
half board mezza pensione 10a
ham prosciutto 10d/12b/12c/13a/13b
hand mano 20e
handbag borsetta 2a
handkerchief fazzoletto 19d
hat cappello 19a
haze foschia 17c
head testa 20d
headache mal di testa 20e
headlights fari 3b
heart attack attacco cardiaco 20d
hello buon giorno 1b, pronto 18c
help aiuto 20g
here qui 5d/6a
here is ecco 1e/6c
high pressure alta pressione 17b
historical building edificio storico 15b
hospital ospedale 20d
hot caldo 17b
hotel albergo, hotel 6a
hour ora 8a
house casa 4b
how come 2c
how much quanto 3c/7b/9d/18b
hurt ferito 20e

English – Italian Vocabulary

husband marito 1f
hydrofoil aliscafo 5c

ice gelo 17d
ice cream gelato 11b/13c
ice cream parlour gelateria 13c
ill malato 20e
indigestion indigestione 20e
information informazione 5e
inn albergo 6a
innocent innocente 20a
insurance assicurazione 20a
island isola 16b
Italian italiano 2c
Italy Italia 2c

jacket giacca 19a
jam marmellata 10c
jug caraffa 10b
juice succo 14a
July luglio 8b

key chiave 1e/1f/6b/20b
kilo chilo 7b
kilometre chilometro 7b
knife coltello 10b
knitwear maglieria 19a

lady donna 1d/19a
lake lago 16b
lamb agnello 12b
last scorso 8c
lawyer avvocato 20c
left sinistra 4d
lemon limone 10c/13c
lemonade limonata 14a
letter lettera 18b
lift ascensore 6b
lighter accendino 14c
like (to) piacere 9c
liqueur liquore 14b
litre litro 3c/7b
little poco 7b
liver fegato 12b
local train treno locale 5a
long lungo 19a
lorry, autocarro 3a

lose (to) perdere 20b
low pressure bassa pressione 17c
luggage bagaglio 1f/2a
lunch pranzo 10a; **to have lunch** pranzare 10a

magazine rivista 2c
main station stazione centrale 5a/7b
man uomo 1d
map carta 4a
market mercato 9c
marmalade marmellata 10c
matches fiammiferi 14c
meat carne 12b
menu menù 11b
metre metro 7b
midday mezzogiorno 8b
midnight mezzanotte 8b
milk latte 10b/14a
mineral water acqua minerale 14a
Miss signorina 1d
moderate moderato 17c
Monday lunedì 8c
money denaro, soldi 9a
month mese 8c
morning mattina, mattino 8b
motorboat motoscafo 16c
motorway autostrada 3b
mountain monte 16b
mountain climbing alpinismo 16c
mountain pass passo 16b
mountains montagna 16b
Mr. signore 1d/6d
Mrs. signora 1d/6d
much molto 1c/7b/17c
municipality comune 4b
museum museo 15b
mushrooms funghi 10d
mussels cozze 12d
my mio 1f

name nome 1f/2b
napkin tovagliolo 10b
narrow stretto 9a
nationality nazionalità 2c
newspaper giornale 2c
next prossimo 8c

English – Italian Vocabulary

night notte 6b/8b
no no 1a/2a
noodles pastasciutta 12a
noon mezzogiorno 8b
not non 1b/2c/9d/20a/20f
note (bank) biglietto 9a
nothing nulla 2a, niente 20f
number numero 6b/18c

occupied occupato 6d
oil olio 3c/11c
ointment pomata 20e
O. K. va bene 2a
olive oliva 13a
one-way street senso unico 3b
onion cipolla 13a
open aperto 15d
open sandwiches tramezzini 10d
opening hours orario 9c/15d
opera opera 15c
orange arancia 13b
origin provenienza 5e
overcast coperto 17c

packet pacchetto 14c
painting quadro 15b
palace palazzo 15b
parking disc disco orario 3d
parking parcheggio 3d
Parmesan cheese parmigiano 12a
passport passaporto 1c/2b
passport control controllo passaporti 2b
pasta pasta 7b/12a
pastries pasticcini 13c
pastry shop pasticceria 11a
peach pesca 10c/13b
peas piselli 13a
pedal boat moscone 16c
pen penna 18b
peninsula penisola 16b
pepper pepe 11c, peperone 13a
performance spettacolo 15c
petrol benzina 3c
photograph (to) fotografare 16d
pill pastiglia 20f
place of residence domicilio 2b

plan (of town) pianta 4a
plaster cerotto 20f
platform binario 5a
plate piatto 16b
please per favore 1c
police polizia, carabinieri 20c
police headquarters questura 20c
pork maiale 12b
port porto 5c
potatoes patate 13a
postbox buca delle lettere 18a
postcard cartolina 18b
post office posta 18a
pound sterling sterlina 9b
prawns gamberi 12d
precipitation precipitazione 17c
press (to) spingere 15d
price prezzo 6c/9d
prohibited vietato 14c/15d
pull (to) tirare 15d
push (to) spingere 15d

quarter quarto 8a/14b
quick presto 20f, subito 20c

railway ferrovia 5a
rain pioggia 17c
rate of exchange cambio 9b
receipt ricevuta 11d
red rosso 19c
rental noleggio 16c
report denuncia 20c
reservation prenotazione 5e
restaurant ristorante, trattoria 11a
return ticket andata e ritorno 5e
rice riso 13a
right destra 4d
river fiume 16b
road strada 3b
roasted arrosto 12c
robbery furto 20b
rockfall caduta massi 3b
roll panino 10c
room camera 6b/10a
rough mosso 17c
rubber dinghy canotto pneumatico 16c

English – Italian Vocabulary

safety belt cintura di sicurezza 20g
sailboard windsurf 16c
salad insalata 13a
salami salame 10d
salt sale 11c
sanitary towels assorbenti 19d
Saturday sabato 8c
sauce sugo, salsa 12b
sea mare 16b/17c
season stazione 8c
seat posto 11a
security control controllo sicurezza 5b
sender mittente 18b
serious grave 20f
service area area di servizio 3b
service station stazione di servizio 3c
shade ombra 17b
shellfish frutti di mare 12d
ship nave 5c
shirt camicia 9c/19a
shoes scarpe 19b
shop negozio 9c
short corto 19a
shower doccia 6b
showers rovesci 17c
shut chiuso 15d
signature firma 2b
single room camera singola 6b
size taglia 19a, misura 19b
ski, skiing sci 16c
ski (to) sciare 16c
skirt gonna 19a
sky cielo 17b
sleep (to) dormire 20e
sleeping car carrozza letti 5a
sleeping pills sonniferi 20f
sleeve manica 19a
slow lento 3a
slow down (to) rallentare 3a
small piccolo 14b
small change spiccioli 9a
snack bar tavola calda 11a
snow neve 17d
snow chain catena da neve 17d
soap sapone 19d
socks calzini 19b
sole sogliola 12d
something qualcosa 2a

soup zuppa, minestra 12a
south sud 4d
sparkling wine spumante 14b
special offer offerta speciale 9c
speed velocità 3a
spinach spinaci 13a
spoon cucchiaio 10b
square piazza, piazzale 4c
squid calamari 12d
stairs scala 6b
stamp francobollo 18b
starter antipasto 2c
station stazione 5a/5d
steak bistecca 12b
steal (to) rubare 20b
stockings calze 19b
stomach stomaco 20e
stomach-ache mal di stomaco 20e
stop fermata 5d
stop alt 4c
straight ahead diritto 4d
strawberries fragole 13b
street via 4c, strada 4d
strong forte 17c
sugar zucchero 11c
suitcase valigia 1e/2a
sun sole 17b
sunburn scottatura solare 20d
Sunday domenica 8c
sunglasses occhiali da sole 19d
suntan cream crema solare 19d
supermarket supermercato 9c
surcharge supplemento 5e
surname cognome 2b
sweater pullover 19a
swim (to) nuotare 16c
swimming pool piscina 16c

table tavola 11a
taxi tassi 5d
tea te 10c/14a
telephone book elenco telefonico 18c
telephone operator centralinista 18c
telephone token gettone 18c
temple tempio 15b
tennis court campo di tennis 16c
terrace terrazza 11a
thank you grazie 1c/9c

English – Italian Vocabulary

the il, la 1e
theatre teatro 15c
there is c'è 1e/6a/17c/20f
there are ci sono 1e
this questo 1e/11d
thunderstorm temporale 17c
Thursday giovedì 8c
ticket biglietto 5e
ticket counter biglietteria 5e
tight stretto 9a
tights collant 19b
time ora 8a
timetable orario 5e
tip mancia 11d
to per 3b/5e/11a/11d
tobacconist tabaccaio, tabaccheria 14c
today oggi 8b/17a
today's menu piatto del giorno 11b
toilet gabinetto 6d
toll charge pedaggio 3b
tomato pomodoro 13a
toothbrush spazzolino da denti 19d
toothpaste dentifricio 19d
tour giro 16a
tourist turista 15a
Tourist Information Bureau azienda di soggiorno 15a
towel asciugamano 19d
tower torre 15b
town-hall comune 4b
traffic light semaforo 4c
train treno 5a
travel agency agenzia di viaggi 15a
trip viaggio 1e/2a, gita 16a
trousers pantaloni 19a
Tuesday martedì 8c
tuna tonno 12d
tunnel galleria 3b
turn on (to) accendere 3b

umbrella ombrello 17c

vacant, free libero 6b/d
valuables articoli di valore 20b

vanilla vaniglia 13c
veal vitello 12b
vegetable verdura 12a/13a
vegetables contorni 13a
vegetable soup minestrone 13a
vehicle veicolo 3a
vermouth vermut 14b
very molto 1c/7b/17c
vinegar aceto 11c
visit (to) visitare 15d
volcano vulcano 16b

waiter cameriere 11d
wallet portafoglio 20b
warm caldo 17b
watch orologio 8a
water acqua 17b
wear abbigliamento 19a
weather tempo 17a/17b/17c
weather forecast previsioni del tempo 17a
Wednesday mercoledì 8c
week settimana 8c
west ovest 4d
what che 8a
when quando 8a/8b
white bianco 9c/19c
wife moglie 1f
wind vento 17c
wine vino 10b/14b
with con 6b/13a/13b/13c/18c
without senza 14c
woman donna 1d/19a
wool lana 19a
work of art opera d'arte 15b

year anno 8c
yellow giallo 19c
yes sì 1a/2c
yesterday ieri 8b
you Lei 11d
your suo 1f
youth hostel ostello della gioventù 6a

Teach Yourself edition first published 1986
Copyright © 1986
Hodder and Stoughton Ltd

Translated and adapted from the original German edition by
Sarah Boas. German edition by Diethard Lübke, copyright ©
1983 by Langenscheidt KG, Berlin and Munich.
Illustrations by Herbert Horn.

British Library Cataloguing in Publication Data

Lubke, Diethard
  Quick and easy Italian.——(Teach yourself books)
  1. Italian language——Spoken Italian
  I. Title
  458.3′421   PC1121

  ISBN 0 340 38767 X

Printed and bound in Great Britain for
Hodder and Stoughton Educational,
a division of Hodder and Stoughton Ltd,
Mill Road, Dunton Green, Sevenoaks, Kent,
Printed in Great Britain by
Fletcher & Son Ltd, Norwich
Typeset by Macmillan India Ltd., Bangalore-25